TV GUIDE

WORD-FIND™

PUZZLES

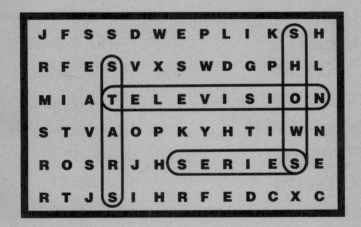

VOLUME 4

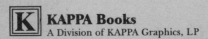

KAPPA Books
A Division of KAPPA Graphics, LP

Monty Python

1. **ANIMATION**
2. **"ARGUMENT Clinic"**
3. **BBC**
4. **"BICYCLE Repairman"**
5. **"The BISHOP"**
6. **"The BLACKMAIL Game"**
7. **Graham CHAPMAN**
8. **"CHEESE Shop"**
9. **John CLEESE**
10. **COMEDY**
11. **"CONFUSE-A-CAT"**
12. **"CRUNCHY Frog"**
13. **ENGLAND**
14. **FARCE**
15. **Terry GILLIAM**
16. **Eric IDLE**
17. **Terry JONES**
18. **"LUMBERJACK Song"**
19. **"NUDGE, NUDGE"**
20. **OUTRAGEOUS**
21. **Michael PALIN**
22. **"Dead PARROT"**
23. **"The PIRANHA Brothers"**
24. **SATIRE**
25. **"SILLY WALKS"**
26. **SKETCHES**
27. **"SPAM"**
28. **"The SPANISH Inquisition"**
29. **SURREAL**
30. **"TWIT of the Year"**
31. **"Arthur 'TWO SHEDS' Jackson"**

```
T A C A E S U F N O C Z Y B R
I R R J G P I B A O T P D M E
F G U R D A R L U R O S E H N
Q U N R U M L T L H C L M S A
O M C Z N A R I S Y C E O C M
Z E H J E A G I A Y W T C N P
T N Y R G N B B C M O A I Z A
Q T R E D I R I V R K L L S H
B U O L U M B E R J A C K K C
S U C D N A A A E P O E A C S
S T W I T T P I P R T N L L K
A H N A R I P N L C I E E H B
S D E H S O W T H L E T R S N
E N G L A N D E H S I N A P S
G A S A N E S E E H C G F S G
```

"SNL" Musical Guests

1. AEROSMITH
2. ALANIS Morissette
3. BETTE Midler
4. BRITNEY Spears
5. CARLY Simon
6. The CARS
7. CHER
8. CLAY Aiken
9. COLDPLAY
10. The CORRS
11. Sheryl CROW
12. DOLLY Parton
13. ELVIS Costello
14. EMINEM
15. EN VOGUE
16. GRATEFUL Dead
17. George HARRISON
18. JET
19. Billy JOEL
20. KYLIE Minogue
21. LENNY Kravitz
22. Jennifer LOPEZ
23. MAROON 5
24. John MAYER
25. Paul MCCARTNEY
26. MOBY
27. Randy NEWMAN
28. NO DOUBT
29. NORAH Jones
30. OUTKAST
31. PATTI Smith
32. Tom PETTY
33. PHISH
34. QUEEN
35. SANTANA
36. Paul SIMON
37. SISQO
38. SPINAL TAP
39. SQUEEZE
40. STEVIE Wonder
41. STING
42. James TAYLOR
43. THE BAND
44. Frank ZAPPA

Word-Find 2

```
P J R Y B Y Y A L C Y L R A C
E E E E N V L G R A T E F U L
I T T N H B L W L A E O W E K
V T E T H C O P Y Z Q J N Y P
E L P R Y R D L E U U V L B H
T Q A A C L O E E Y O I P R I
S M T C O R U E Z G E L V I S
A P T C N Q N O U T K A S T H
H T I M S O R E A O S T I N G
A B H N A R S Z W N Q Z E E N
R U L E A Y A I E M A S M Y N
O O A Y B L E C R P A T I I O
N D B J Q A T R P R O N N S M
C O R R S I N A L A A L E A I
M N O O R A M D P K J H M V S
```

Homer Jay Simpson

1. ABRAHAM (father)
2. ASTRONAUT
3. BART (son)
4. "BE SHARPS"
5. BODYGUARD
6. BOWLER
7. BOXER
8. BROKEN bones
9. CARNY
10. Dan CASTELLANETA (voice)
11. CLERK
12. CRAYON in brain
13. Food CRITIC
14. "DANCIN' Homer"
15. "D'OH"
16. DOUGHNUTS
17. DUFF Beer
18. GRIFTER
19. "HOMEY"
20. LISA (daughter)
21. MAGGIE (daughter)
22. MARGE (wife)
23. MASCOT
24. MATT Groening (creator)
25. "MAX POWER"
26. MISSIONARY
27. "MR. PLOW"
28. "MR. X"
29. MUSICIAN
30. NUCLEAR power plant
31. "POOCHIE"
32. SAFETY inspector
33. SALESMAN
34. SANTA Claus
35. SPRINGFIELD
36. "TOMACCO"
37. TRUCKER

Word-Find 3

```
M R P L O W C S O C C A M O T
R E W N H L A I M A T T I H R
A W R O A L L F T E Y I S O A
E O D L E I F G N I R P S M B
L P M S S U C A N R R R I E T
C X M A D I L I E O E C O Y R
U A C J G L S T S X Y D N N N
N M S L E G F P O U O A A R I
P G Y T E I I B R U M L R A C
O S S D R R R E G A V A Y C N
O A Y G U O K H M A H A R B A
C F N U K C N A T N A S M G D
H E Z E U U B A B O W L E R E
I T N R T D R A U G Y D O B X
E Y T S M A S C O T Q W S C K
```

Favorite Newscasters

1. Christiane AMANPOUR
2. Ashleigh BANFIELD
3. Maria BARTIROMO
4. David BRINKLEY
5. Kent BROCKMAN
6. Tom BROKAW
7. Aaron BROWN
8. Earl CAMERON
9. Connie CHUNG
10. Walter CRONKITE
11. Ann CURRY
12. Laurie DHUE
13. Sam DONALDSON
14. Bob EDWARDS
15. Brit HUME
16. Chet HUNTLEY
17. Peter JENNINGS
18. Ted KOPPEL
19. Jim LEHRER
20. Robert MACNEIL
21. Trevor MCDONALD
22. Arthel NEVILLE
23. Edwin NEWMAN
24. Deborah NORVILLE
25. Jane PAULEY
26. Dan RATHER
27. Angela RIPPON
28. Tim RUSSERT
29. Jessica SAVITCH
30. Maria SHRIVER
31. Peter SISSONS
32. Brian WILLIAMS
33. Paula ZAHN

Word-Find 4

```
R N B G N U H C T I V A S E L
A M A N P O U R P P B X M Y N
T I N M K S S N E T A U A B Y
H Y F G K V S D H E H U I E I
E R I C S C W I L N B P L O G
R R E X G A O L S A A K L E H
F U L N R W I R R S N M I F Y
X C D D O V E T B I O O W Y J
L E S Z R R I U R R V N D E E
I U A O H R E B O E O P S L N
E H N E O P R M K N V W L T N
N D L M C D O N A L D I N N I
C R O N K I T E W C V L R U N
A I Y T C R U S S E R T K H G
M S L E P P O K N O P P I R S
```

"Reno 911!"

1. CARLOS Alazraqui
2. CEDRIC Yarbrough
3. CHARACTERS
4. Deputy CLEMENTINE Johnson
5. COMEDY
6. COPS
7. Lt. Jim DANGLE
8. DEPUTIES
9. Robert Ben GARANT
10. Deputy GARCIA
11. IMPROV
12. IRREVERENT
13. Deputy JONES
14. Deputy Travis JUNIOR
15. KERRI Kenney-Silver
16. Thomas LENNON
17. MUSTACHES
18. NEVADA
19. NIECY Nash
20. PARODY
21. RENO
22. SATIRE
23. SHERIFFS
24. SUNGLASSES
25. Deputy TRUDY Wiegel
26. UNIFORMS
27. WENDI McLendon-Covey
28. Deputy WILLIAMS

Word-Find 5

```
S F F I R E H S V J I M Y H S
J W E N D I C S N K U K V X Y
N I K J S S M H E S E L L D C
I R R E K R O P T N O B E S A
X I H Q O G E A R K O M N E R
F N R F A R C T P O O J N I L
Y T I R I H L P C C V N O T O
C N C T E S E S S A L G N U S
U I A S J V M Y D O R A P P W
A S V C L U E A M A O A H E F
O P Y I T I N R I N D F H D Y
S G A R A N T I E L A A X C C
J P U D U K I R O N L L V Q E
K D O E L G N A D R T I I E I
Y R G C Z T E D U Q F V W S N
```

The Fonz

1. "AAAYYH"
2. APARTMENT
3. ARNOLD'S Drive-In
4. ARTHUR Fonzarelli
5. BACHELOR
6. BRONCO'S Auto Repairs
7. CHACHI
8. "CHICKS"
9. COOL
10. COUSIN
11. CUNNINGHAM family
12. DIPLOMA
13. The FALCONS
14. FONZARELLI
15. JOANIE
16. JUKEBOX
17. LEATHER jacket
18. LONER
19. MEN'S room office
20. MILWAUKEE
21. MOTORCYCLE
22. "MR. C."
23. NIGHT school
24. PALS
25. PINKY Tuscadero
26. POTSIE
27. RALPH
28. RICHIE
29. Jumped a SHARK
30. SHOP teacher
31. "SHORTCAKE"
32. THUMBS up
33. Henry WINKLER

Word-Find 6

```
C T L V R C B N K E L M R J F
S H E F E E O U L R R O H B V
B G A K L H L C H C A I N R P
M I T C A B Y K P R L H P E P
U N H X H C R O N L P O S I R
H J E U R I T O E I H I N N S
T F R O V S L R N S W K S A P
N U T D I D A B O C Y N A O A
E O N E S Z Q U A H O K F J L
M A H G N I N N U C S S C U S
T B C O U S I N L B H J N K V
R R F M I L W A U K E E C E E
A A A Y Y H F M I V Q I L B M
P Y A R T H U R I C H I E O Q
A M O L P I D O E C O O L X R
```

1. AARON'S Way
2. ABBY
3. ADAM 12
4. The ADDAMS Family
5. ADDERLY
6. The AGENCY
7. AIRWOLF
8. ALF
9. ALIAS
10. ALICE
11. ALKALI Ike
12. ALL IN the Family
13. ALLY McBeal
14. ALMOST Perfect
15. AMANDA'S
16. AMEN
17. AMERICAN Bandstand
18. AMY Prentiss
19. The ANDY Griffith Show
20. ANGEL
21. ANGIE
22. ANY DAY NOW
23. ARCHER
24. ARNIE
25. ARSENIO
26. AS IF
27. The ASSOCIATES
28. The A-TEAM
29. AT EASE
30. AUTOMAN
31. The AVENGERS

Word-Find 7

```
K R M C C I W A U T O M A N L
S E T A I C O S S A H D A E R
C P R A E Q N O R J D G G E H
A S I F I T Y A E E E E I P R
O I N E S R A L R N G I M D E
Q K R B J H D L C S R N D F H
G J M W N I Y Y Y V Z R E U C
T B Y E O U N N M W D A C V R
Q S M B T L A M A J C V H S A
K A O F B C F T S N O R A A E
E D G M I A N G E L D L S D X
I D L R L I N C R A K Y A N P
G A E S L A I A O A S L D A P
N M W L S L E T L I F E A M I
A S A H A S A I L A M A D A Y
```

1. When PAMELA
2. ANDERSON Lee
3. LEFT
4. "BAYWATCH,"
5. she TOOK her
6. FANS to a
7. NEW
8. ADVENTURE
9. SERIES called
10. "V.I.P."
11. Pam PLAYED
12. VALLERY
13. IRONS, the
14. HEAD of
15. COLT
16. ARROW
17. SECURITY
18. SERVICES,
19. RENAMED in
20. her HONOR.
21. SHE and
22. her TEAM —
23. TASHA,
24. NIKKI,
25. QUICK,
26. JOHNNY,
27. MAXINE,
28. and KAY —
29. SOLVED
30. many CASES.
31. IT WAS
32. "MISSION:
33. IMPOSSIBLE"
34. MEETS
35. "CHARLIE'S
36. ANGELS."

Word-Find 8

```
S S V D P S S K I K K I N S K
E P A M E L A H C T A W Y A B
C I D S E A A H E I F F Y R J
I V A D N E A Y R K U E H R U
V C Q G Z R T T E A M Q L O N
R W E N L R R S M D R F C W J
E L B I S S O P M I T N M E X
S R E C F A N S J N S A Z V D
E S U D D B O J O E X S S A E
C S E T N S H S H I Z T I H M
U A O I N M R D N O B V K O A
R W Z O R E A E N O C H H K N
I T R L D E V R Y M O H O E E
T I Y N H R S D E V L O S A R
Y E A Y R E L L A V T G X A N
```

1. **CLORIS**

2. **LEACHMAN**

3. has **BEEN**

4. **ACTIVE**

5. **IN TV**

6. **SINCE** its

7. early **DAYS,**

8. **APPEARING**

9. in **TWELVE**

10. **REGULAR**

11. **SERIES** and

12. in **MANY**

13. **DRAMA**

14. **SHOWS.**

15. **SHE'S** been

16. a **GUEST**

17. on **NUMEROUS**

18. **PROGRAMS,**

19. **INCLUDING**

20. "The **SIMPSONS."**

21. She has **WON**

22. **SEVEN**

23. **EMMYS** for

24. her **WORK,** on

25. shows **SUCH AS**

26. "**PROMISED**

27. **LAND"** and

28. "**MALCOLM** in

29. the **MIDDLE."**

Word-Find 9

```
D S H O W S A T S H E S W Q N
N Z E B W S S M B D Y U S D C
A J L V T W N E A M M C Z V B
M W G T E D C O M R E H P E M
H J U N H N Y E S Y D A R L M
C R E I I A O Y R P C S O D F
A I S S L L A W R T M C M D T
E P T E F D O O I Z L I I I X
L L P C I R G V S A T D S M V
P I B E K R E X M E V L E W T
C F N E A M E G V P Q K D R S
O E W M E R S S U G H F W M V
N O S R G N I D U L C N I Q E
Y N A M N G W N Y I A Z L Y E
S U O R E M U N G S I R O L C
```

"The Brady Bunch"

1. ALICE Nelson
2. ARCHITECT
3. BOBBY
4. BRADY
5. CAROL
6. CINDY
7. Imogene COCA
8. CULT favorite
9. DAVY JONES
10. DEACON Jones
11. DESI Arnaz, Jr.
12. DON HO
13. Don DRYSDALE
14. FAMILY
15. GRAND CANYON
16. GREG
17. HAWAII
18. JAN
19. "JOHNNY BRAVO"
20. LESSONS
21. MAID
22. MARCIA
23. MIKE
24. Joe NAMATH
25. Cousin OLIVER
26. PETER
27. SAM the Butcher
28. SHERWOOD Schwartz
29. SIX kids
30. THEME SONG
31. TIGER
32. VINCENT Price

Word-Find 10

```
I  I  G  G  E  G  P  G  L  B  N  S  P  I  A
R  M  R  K  Y  N  X  N  T  O  N  E  V  F  L
D  E  I  I  A  W  A  H  Y  O  T  L  S  O  V
G  M  G  R  W  M  P  N  S  E  N  A  R  Z  Q
J  E  K  I  A  L  A  S  R  T  E  A  G  H  I
D  O  L  T  T  C  E  T  I  H  C  R  A  F  S
I  E  H  A  D  L  D  I  D  E  N  Z  M  A  S
A  J  S  N  D  H  Y  A  R  M  I  J  F  U  I
M  M  A  I  N  S  V  B  C  E  V  E  A  U  X
B  R  A  D  Y  Y  Y  A  B  S  V  C  M  N  S
G  D  O  R  J  J  B  R  J  O  W  I  I  L  N
X  H  H  O  C  I  Q  R  D  N  B  L  L  C  V
Y  D  N  I  C  I  E  W  A  G  O  A  Y  O  J
T  E  O  N  O  C  A  E  D  V  T  L  U  C  Z
S  D  D  G  P  S  H  E  R  W  O  O  D  A  K
```

TV GUIDE WORD-FINDS

TV GUIDE

TV Cities and Towns

1. BEDROCK
2. CABOT COVE
3. CAPESIDE
4. CICELY
5. EERIE
6. FERNWOOD
7. HOOTERVILLE
8. MAYBERRY
9. MAYFIELD
10. METROPOLIS
11. MOOSESYL-
    VANIA
12. NORWICH
13. PALMERSTOWN
14. PEYTON PLACE
15. PORT CHARLES
16. RIVERSIDE
17. SALEM
18. SMALLVILLE
19. SPRINGFIELD
20. STUCKEYVILLE
21. SUNNYDALE
22. TWIN PEAKS
23. WALNUT GROVE

Word-Find 11

```
R S P A L M E R S T O W N K E
G I E V O R G T U N L A W P Q
M L Y N I E H K C O R D E B F
D O T D H U D L E I F Y A M O
O P O S Z O O I V O E B E A P
O O N S P F O E S L A L B Y O
W R P C E R R T A E L G V B R
N T L T A S I D E I P H C E T
R E A E I B Y N V R O A I R C
E M C D I N O L G V V X C R H
F E E N N R L T V F Z I E Y A
V L Q U W A E W C A I L L Y R
V A S I M M F E C O N E Y L L
Q S C S T U C K E Y V I L L E
U H S K A E P N I W T E A D S
```

TV GUIDE WORD-FINDS

"South Park"

1. ANIMATION
2. Officer BARBRADY
3. BLEEPS
4. BUTTERS
5. Eric CARTMAN
6. CHEF
7. CHILDREN
8. COLORADO
9. Mrs. CRABTREE
10. CURRENT events
11. GRANDPA Marsh
12. KENNY McCormick
13. KYLE Broslofski
14. LANGUAGE
15. MATT Stone (creator)
16. MAYOR McDaniels
17. Dr. MEPHESTO
18. Kyle's MOM
19. MR. GARRISON
20. MR. HAT
21. NURSE Gollum
22. PHILIP
23. PIP Pirrup
24. PRINCIPAL Victoria
25. RACY
26. SONGS
27. STAN Marsh
28. TERRANCE
29. TIMMY
30. TOWN
31. TREY Parker (creator)
32. TWEEK
33. WENDY Testaberger

Word-Find 12

```
C X U I D R A N I M A T I O N
Q O B A P D N A R G O T Q B E
K Y L E T N E G B U A M N G R
L W E O D T A T A H L Y A Y D
Q A E J R R A K R A C U M S L
Q S P N R A C M B A G M T K I
I G S I D D D R R N I A R U H
R N S P C Y M O A T N O A N C
R O Y A M N S L D B T N C U H
N S N W O T I R Y S T W R R E
G Y E C N A R R E T Y R E S F
Q V I S J V A H P T E E E E W
O P H I L I P J Z N T I R E K
G I Y N N E K C T T Q U U T M
B P Q I M L M Q U Z I T B Q E
```

Steven Bochco

1. "BAY CITY Blues"
2. CARNEGIE Tech
3. "COLUMBO"
4. "COP ROCK"
5. "The COUNTERFEIT Killer"
6. DAYNA (wife)
7. DECEMBER birthday
8. "DELVECCHIO"
9. EMMY Awards
10. "GRIFF"
11. "HILL STREET Blues"
12. "HOOPERMAN"
13. "Doogie HOWSER, M.D."
14. "L.A. LAW"
15. "MURDER ONE"
16. NEW YORK
17. "NYPD BLUE"
18. "OPERATING Room"
19. "PARIS"
20. "PHILLY"
21. SERBIAN heritage
22. "SILENT Running"
23. STEVAN Bozovic
24. "TOTAL Security"
25. UNIVERSAL Television
26. New York UNIVERSITY
27. "Lt. Shuster's WIFE"

Word-Find 13

```
S I R A P C C K Y L C Z D U S
F H O O P E R M A N K H A D K
F F I R G O T S G T S A Y U E
T J G L Y T R J N V T O N W U
H Q U W L E O E I L E I A V N
G O E K V S L T T D V L Y F K
O N W I C I T C A E A L T V M
S B N S S O A R R L N O I E U
Y U M M E R R S E V K C C F R
G L E U N R I P P E M M Y I D
K A L E L T M C O C T U A W E
G U G I Y O X D E C E M B E R
K I M W H T C A N H Q Z Y F O
E U L B D P Y N A I B R E S N
T I E F R E T N U O C N Z I E
```

TV GUIDE WORD-FINDS

"Star Trek" Voice-Over

1. SPACE:

2. THE FINAL

3. FRONTIER.

4. THESE

5. ARE the

6. VOYAGES of

7. the STARSHIP

8. "ENTERPRISE."

9. Its FIVE-

10. YEAR

11. MISSION:

12. TO EXPLORE

13. STRANGE

14. NEW

15. WORLDS;

16. TO SEEK

17. OUT new

18. LIFE

19. AND new

20. CIVILIZATIONS;

21. TO BOLDLY

22. GO WHERE

23. NO MAN

24. HAS

25. GONE

26. BEFORE.

Word-Find 14

```
T  J  U  F  F  I  W  E  N  I  B  X  S  D  H
O  M  J  C  X  I  R  S  X  A  Q  I  Y  M  T
S  E  G  A  Y  O  V  L  G  S  D  T  C  I  X
E  J  J  R  F  L  A  E  R  P  D  I  H  S  F
E  E  Y  E  P  N  W  T  V  L  V  L  C  S  C
K  C  B  C  I  E  C  P  K  I  Y  U  R  I  G
F  H  S  F  H  I  S  Y  L  D  L  O  B  O  T
L  R  E  T  S  S  L  I  F  E  G  G  W  N  W
C  H  O  F  R  N  Z  G  R  O  N  H  I  E  V
T  P  Y  N  A  A  W  B  N  P  E  R  S  C  H
T  P  C  M  T  B  N  E  Y  R  R  A  G  A  G
H  U  O  I  S  I  E  G  E  C  J  E  S  P  E
D  N  O  C  T  H  E  S  E  V  Z  Y  T  S  J
W  N  V  K  C  W  S  R  I  T  U  E  H  N  Z
S  B  A  X  V  O  T  O  E  X  P  L  O  R  E
```

Top Shows: 1953

1. AT ISSUE
2. BONINO
3. Our Miss BROOKS
4. Beat the CLOCK
5. Make Room for DADDY
6. DANGER
7. DOWN You Go
8. DRAGNET
9. ETHEL & Albert
10. FORD Theatre
11. I LOVE LUCY
12. JAMIE
13. JUDGE for Yourself
14. LETTER to Loretta
15. The LONE RANGER
16. MAMA
17. My Little MARGIE
18. MEET Millie
19. MELODY Street
20. MR. PEEPERS
21. MR. WIZARD
22. NAME That Tune
23. See It NOW
24. PERSON to Person
25. PLACE the Face
26. QUIZ Kids
27. The Life of RILEY
28. ROCKY King, Detective
29. I've Got a SECRET
30. Your Show of SHOWS
31. SKY KING
32. Comeback STORY
33. SUSPENSE
34. THIS Is Your Life
35. TOPPER
36. Big TOWN
37. TWENTY Questions
38. The WEB
39. WHAT'S My Line
40. WHO Said That?
41. YOU BET Your Life

Word-Find 15

```
E T T Y O U B E T W E N T Y R
N O I E K N U O T H I S K E E
W O N L N C I G N I K Y K S G
O F T P O G O N P O M A N L N
D R O F N V A R O J M E A E A
M R P E E P E R S B P Y E T R
R J P M S D B L D S E Z I T E
W A E T A E B Z U L J S G E N
I M R N M M C S I C S T R R O
Z I G A E B A R I U Y O A L L
A E N L N O S R E P Q R M E W
R G O E T W P H V T L Y P H X
D D A D D Y K C O L C A A T B
Y U P M Y K R W H W S T C E C
M J J L W P N U W V S A W E S
```

TV GUIDE WORD-FINDS

1. Eric's BASEMENT
2. BOB
3. DISCO era
4. DONNA
5. ERIC
6. EXCHANGE student
7. FES
8. FORMAN family
9. FRIENDS
10. GRADUATION
11. HYDE
12. JACKIE
13. KELSO
14. KITTY
15. LAURIE
16. LEISURE suits
17. LEO
18. LONG hair
19. Price MART
20. MIDGE
21. NEIGHBORS
22. NINETEEN seventy-six
23. NURSE
24. POINT Place
25. RED
26. ROMANCES
27. High SCHOOL
28. SEVENTIES
29. Platform SHOES
30. SITCOM
31. Appliance STORE
32. STUDENTS
33. SUBURBS
34. WISCONSIN

Word-Find 16

```
O M S J O F D I S C O D L T M
Y O H D E R I W E U U I V L I
A C O B L N U R S E B T T I D
T T E D G W I F U P I U S G G
N I S N O C S I W L A U R I E
E S N E E T E N I N W A S B B
I S D A V I S T E Z D E E S S
G Y T K M E A G N U F E C T T
H E S N R R N N A I Y H N Q N
B R K O E A O T N E O E A B N
O U T I H D I F I O M P M M H
R S C C T O U K L E D L O M P
S I X B N T C T S O S O R A M
K E L S O A Y A S D N E I R F
W L X A J B B I C F M G C T Q
```

"Missing"

1. ABILITIES
2. Vivica A. FOX
3. Special AGENTS
4. ANTONIO
5. CATERINA Scorsone
6. CLUES
7. CONSULTANT
8. DANGERS
9. Assistant DIRECTOR
10. EVIDENCE
11. FBI
12. GIFTED
13. IDEALISM
14. INVESTIGATE
15. INVOLVED
16. JESS
17. JOHN
18. JUSTIN Louis
19. LONG hours
20. MARK Consuelos
21. MISSING persons
22. NEW partner
23. NICOLE
24. PSYCHIC
25. RESULTS
26. ROOKIE
27. SLEEP
28. SOLVE cases
29. TASK force
30. TEAM
31. TITLE change
32. TRAINING
33. VISIONS
34. WITNESSES

Word-Find 17

```
D M T A S K M C Z L E W E D Y
C X P B I I N R A J I H V E A
T R A I N I N G O T E E L V S
F S T L U S E R N T E S O L T
I R S I C O J E J O C R S O N
T N A T L U S N O C L E I V E
E I V I U S V I G Z C G R N G
A C Q E E I N I P N M N L I A
M O A S S O F S E N H A E G D
Q L I L T T Y D N O I D R W E
T E E N E C I K J O G T V K O
W E A D H V R G G N I S S I M
P P M I E I D E A L I S M U S
L R C J B E L T I T W X I V J
Q X O F A R O O K I E G H V E
```

TV GUIDE WORD-FINDS

Bruce Boxleitner

1. Mary Kay ADAMS
2. Edward ALBERT
3. ANDREA Thompson
4. James ARNESS
5. "BABYLON 5"
6. Richard BIGGS
7. BILL Mumy
8. Raleigh BOND
9. "BRING 'Em Back Alive"
10. CAITLIN Brown
11. CINDY Morgan
12. CLYDE Kusatsu
13. William Kirby CULLEN
14. DEBORAH Raffin
15. Jerry DOYLE
16. Stephen FURST
17. Beverly GARLAND
18. Sharon GLESS
19. GREG Morton
20. Kate JACKSON
21. KATHRYN Holcomb
22. KIM Darby
23. "The LAST Convertible"
24. MARTHA Smith
25. MEL Stewart
26. MYRON Natwick
27. Michael NOURI
28. Michael O'HARE
29. PAUL Stout
30. PERRY King
31. "SCARECROW and Mrs. King"
32. SEAN McClory
33. John SHEA
34. VICKI Schreck
35. "How the WEST Was Won"
36. John ZEE

Word-Find 18

```
N E L L U C N O S K C A J L P
Q M O F J G F C L S E L Q K W
V Z D Q U P A N L U S B O N D
S S E L G R O R Y A W E I O S
M Z B K E L S R L E S R N U H
A E O C Y U C T S A E T S R E
D K R B C A I T L I N L F I A
A O A S I K C I V J I D Y B E
W B H N D L L I B M D R O R
H I X A Y R R E P E N I A O D
I G L D R R F G N I N H K K N
U G E U N E H E C G T V G O A
V S H U A X P T R R M H R E C
A H U C E P T E A F G Y O E C
F K U O S W G M K K M E L Z B
```

1. "The ADDAMS Family"
2. "Charlie's ANGELS"
3. "BARETTA"
4. "BARNEY Miller"
5. "BEWITCHED"
6. "CHEYENNE"
7. "All My CHILDREN"
8. "COMBAT"
9. "Three's COMPANY"
10. FRED Silverman
11. "GENERAL Hospital"
12. "HAPPY DAYS"
13. Peter JENNINGS
14. "Welcome Back, KOTTER"
15. "LAVERNE & Shirley"
16. LEONARD Goldenson
17. "The LOVE BOAT"
18. "MCHALE'S NAVY"
19. "MONDAY Night Football"
20. "MORK & Mindy"
21. "MY THREE SONS"
22. "OPERATION Petticoat"
23. "PEYTON Place"
24. "RICH MAN, Poor Man"
25. ROONE Arledge
26. "ROOTS"
27. "RYAN'S HOPE"
28. "The SIX MILLION Dollar Man"
29. "TAXI"
30. Barbara WALTERS
31. "Marcus WELBY, M.D."

Word-Find 19

```
A D D A M S V O S R E T L A W
O A S A Y V A N S E L A H C M
B E W I T C H E D X R Y H H A
K N A M H C I R E E X A I E T
L A V E R N E P N B P X Y Y T
O M N R E I O E E P A N Z E E
L O O O E H G I Y T A R J N R
E N I O S T S D L P A Y N N A
O D T N O A A G M L E B R E B
N A A E N Y M O N Y I Y M W Y
A Y R G S Z C O B I B M T O S
R T E C H I L D R E N L X O C
D L P L W H E O B K V N E I N
S T O O R R E T T O K O E W S
N I P M F S Q M Q D A N L J B
```

TV GUIDE

TV GUIDE WORD-FINDS

Through the Years: CBS

1. Winston BURDETT
2. BURNS and Allen
3. CBS EVENING NEWS
4. CBS RESEARCH Center
5. Charles COLLINGWOOD
6. Walter CRONKITE
7. ED SULLIVAN
8. "All in the FAMILY"
9. Arthur GODFREY
10. Peter GOLDMARK
11. "GUNSMOKE"
12. HOWARD K. Smith
13. IKE AND LEON Levy
14. Richard K. HOTTELET
15. David LETTERMAN
16. William L. SHIRER
17. "M*A*S*H"
18. "The Mary Tyler MOORE Show"
19. William PALEY
20. Columbia PHONOGRAPH Company
21. Dan RATHER
22. RED SKELTON
23. Edward R. MURROW
24. Eric SEVAREID
25. Fred SILVERMAN
26. Dr. Frank STANTON
27. WESTINGHOUSE Corporation

Word-Find 20

```
X P G D I E T I K N O R C S S
G G H O W A R D K R M B R E T
R K H O T T E L E T S E N V A
M R W S N L S H I R E R O A N
U A E D N O T L E K S D E R T
R P S B O A G S B M Y N L E O
R K T H R O E R E U A E D I N
O R I R G A W K A V R N N D A
W A N E R O O G I P Y D A K M
H M G C R M D L N L H A E X R
B D H O S O L F I I F J K T E
U L O N Q U O M R F L A I X T
R O U K S N A M R E V L I S T
N G S D D F P A L E Y Z O D E
S W E N G N I N E V E S B C L
```

1. National BROADCASTING Company
2. Johnny CARSON
3. "CHEERS"
4. CNBC
5. "The COSBY SHOW"
6. General ELECTRIC
7. EMPIRE State Building
8. "FAMILY TIES"
9. "FRASIER"
10. "FRIENDS"
11. "HILL STREET Blues"
12. Robert KINTNER
13. "KRAFT Television Theater"
14. Warren LITTLEFIELD
15. MADE-FOR-TV movies
16. MCA-UNIVERSAL
17. "MCCLOUD"
18. "MCMILLAN and Wife"
19. "The NBC MYSTERY Movie"
20. "PETER PAN"
21. RADIO Corporation of America
22. RESEARCH
23. "ST. ELSEWHERE"
24. Brandon TARTIKOFF
25. Grant TINKER
26. "TODAY"
27. "TONIGHT"
28. "The VIRGINIAN"
29. Sylvester "Pat" WEAVER

Word-Find 21

```
D G I O I X D U O L C C M W C
E A Q W O H S Y B S O C E T A
Y R E T S Y M C B N A A O Y R
H R E I S A R F S U V N S Q S
C T W H F I R L N E I E T T O
R E F Z W I V I R G I N I A N
A E K A E E V T H T A Z N R A
E R R N R E S T Y P A D K T L
S T D I R K L L R C T I E I L
E S O S P E I E E O N F R K I
R L A D N M T F C T F B W O M
Z L J S A E E I N T S E C F C
W I P F P Y Y E Y M R B D F M
C H E E R S R L R A D I O A X
G N I T S A C D A O R B C H M
```

TV GUIDE WORD-FINDS

TV GUIDE

"Clean Sweep"

1. ANGELO Surmelis
2. BEDROOM
3. CARPENTER
4. CHARITY
5. CLOSETS
6. CLUTTER
7. CREATIVE
8. Two DAYS
9. DESIGNER
10. DISORDER
11. DRAMATIC
12. EMOTIONS
13. ERIC Stromer
14. FUNCTIONAL
15. HOST
16. LIVING room
17. MOLLY Leutkemeyer
18. MONEY
19. OFFICE
20. ORGANIZER
21. PAINTING
22. PETER Walsh
23. PRICING
24. PROFESSIONALS
25. QUICK decisions
26. SHELLI Alexander
27. SOLUTIONS
28. SPACE
29. STACEY Dutton
30. TAVA Smiley
31. TEAM
32. TIPS
33. TRANSFORMA-TION
34. TWO areas
35. VALERIE Bickford
36. YARD sale

Word-Find 22

```
E I R E L A V U Q U I C K L X
N T F G N I V I L L E H S X O
O O V C M M Y A R D T A I F C
Q L I D R A M A T I C R F L L
R R E T N E P R A C O I U A O
E G Q G A T N E B R C T N E S
T N E S N M C G G E T Y C M E
E I V S O A R A I E D R T O T
P T I J P L N O R S E R I T S
Y N T S P I U I F D E O O I O
E I A I Z T T T R S M D N O H
N A E E W S E O I U N O A N M
O P R O F E S S I O N A L S T
M O C G N I C I R P N P R L Q
W S Y A D J Y E C A T S U T Y
```

Making a Living

1. "ALICE"

2. WAITRESS;

3. "BAYWATCH"

4. LIFEGUARD;

5. "BOSTON Public"

6. TEACHER;

7. "CHICAGO Hope"

8. DOCTOR;

9. "The FALL GUY"

10. STUNTMAN;

11. "FRASIER"

12. PSYCHIATRIST;

13. "LOU GRANT"

14. JOURNALIST;

15. "MATLOCK"

16. LAWYER;

17. "The Real

MCCOYS"

18. FARMER;

19. "NEWHART"

20. INNKEEPER;

21. "NYPD Blue"

22. DETECTIVE;

23. "Gomer PYLE,

USMC"

24. MARINE;

25. "SEINFELD"

26. COMEDIAN;

27. "WANTED: Dead

or Alive"

28. BOUNTY hunter;

29. "WINGS"

30. PILOT.

Word-Find 23

```
N O T S O B V S E I N F E L D
L T O S L C L O D A S W O E O
S S L T I Q W O G T X Y T R C
W R I R F R V A U A U E E X T
I E P A E S T N I G C M T F O
N P B H G K T A L T R I R B R
G E A W U M B L I A R A H Q E
S E Y E A U A V F H K E N C H
Y K W N R F E D B K C F S T C
O N A I D E M O C O R Y Y S A
C N T L J O U R N A L I S T E
C I C E I N C M S U E L Y P T
M Q H B T C Y I K C O L T A M
L A W Y E R E P A M L T U V M
N G E N I R A M D E T N A W S
```

A Noble Experiment

1. NINETEEN
2. NINETY'S
3. "COP
4. ROCK"
5. BOASTED
6. an ESTEEMED
7. GROUP of
8. ACTORS and
9. an ORIGINAL
10. IDEA:
11. A MUSICAL
12. POLICE
13. DRAMA,
14. with BOTH
15. HEROES and
16. PERPS
17. WAILING
18. out TUNES.
19. BARBARA
20. BOSSON, of
21. "HILL Street
22. BLUES"
23. FAME,
24. HEADED up
25. the CAST,
26. which ALSO
27. FEATURED
28. JAMES
29. MCDANIEL,
30. PAUL
31. MCCRANE,
32. and TERI
33. AUSTIN.
34. ALAS, the
35. SERIES
36. LASTED
37. LESS than
38. two MONTHS.

Word-Find 24

```
T A J A M E S S E O R E H C B
P U O R G C Y K C O R T F C B
T S N X Z T C I E S L L A L D
E T E E E S E R I E S S U E S
H I C N S M B O A S T E D A A
G N I L I A W K W N S A L N P
J N L X G M E S T E E M E D Z
I I O A P U C C X H B E T F A
H E P R N S B D D B T M E X O
C J E A O I R H A E O A R F Z
I O R B S C G O N N T T I A A
K J P R S A M I T U I S H M L
W S S A O L N H R C W E A E S
Q A L B B W S E P O A R L L O
J A C B D U D E A E D I A Y M
```

Hi Neighbor!

1. The BUNDYS
2. and MARCY;
3. the BUNKERS
4. and the JEFFERSONS;
5. the CLAMPETTS
6. and the DRYSDALES;
7. DENNIS
8. and the WILSONS;
9. the FLINTSTONES
10. and the RUBBLES;
11. JERRY Seinfeld
12. and KRAMER;
13. the KEATONS
14. and SKIPPY;
15. the KRAMDENS
16. and the NORTONS;
17. the RICARDOS
18. and the MERTZES;
19. the SANFORDS
20. and JULIO;
21. the SIMPSONS
22. and Ned FLANDERS;
23. the WINSLOWS
24. and URKEL.

Word-Find 25

```
S M O E S O D R A C I R G D H
E K I M I N J S E Z T R E M S
N W L S K L O B N Y N N Q A C
O I U A A D U S H O N W C R Q
T L J Z E N R H R I S J L C O
S S T F K E F W S E E P A Y F
T O W E D V I O N R F L M I B
N N R N U N K O R D X F P I Z
I S A L S D R Y S D A L E S S
L L W L R T A S T K S Y T J E
F K O L O V M B Y H R F T O L
A W B N E Z D F O D R A S N B
S L S M N K E A T O N S M N B
G E K I Q T N L E K R U S E U
I Y P P I K S V M P T Q B G R
```

TV GUIDE WORD-FINDS

"Route 66"

1. ADVENTURE series
2. ANTHOLOGY
3. BORIS Karloff
4. BUSTER Keaton
5. BUZ
6. Lon CHANEY, JR.
7. Glenn CORBETT
8. CORVETTE
9. Joan CRAWFORD
10. CROSS-COUNTRY
11. DRAMA
12. Robert DUVALL
13. ENCOUNTERS
14. GUEST stars
15. LINC
16. LOCATIONS
17. Peter LORRE
18. George MAHARIS
19. Martin MILNER
20. NOMADS
21. ON THE ROAD
22. Suzanne PLESHETTE
23. Robert REDFORD
24. SIXTIES
25. STATES
26. STOPS
27. THEME SONG
28. TOD
29. U.S. HIGHWAY 66

```
J S O A M A R D Y S T A T E S
C V E N O B O A R E D F O R D
O H P I T T W N H M W S B U Z
Y N A E T H E M E S O N G T T
Y R N N G X E E Z G D O R N R
S I T I E M I R B R W I E E J
Z T H N A Y T S O P K T T V H
D S O A U S J F R A T A S D E
U I L P E O W R C E D C U A H
V R O U S A C O H N N O B I C
A A G F R Y R S H M O L N N B
L H Y C V B E L S X R M I N O
L A C B E L E R R O L L A M R
D M N T P E T T E V R O C D I
J W T K S R E T N U O C N E S
```

"Ryan's Hope"

1. Nancy ADDISON
2. Bernard BARROW
3. BOB
4. BUCKY
5. Faith CATLIN
6. Working CLASS
7. CLEM
8. DELIA
9. EARL Hindman
10. EDMUND
11. FAITH
12. Ryan FAMILY
13. FRANK
14. Ron HALE
15. HANNIBAL Penney
16. Michael HAWKINS
17. HELEN Gallagher
18. JACK
19. JILLIAN
20. JOHNNY
21. JUSTIN Deas
22. William KIEHL
23. Ilene KRISTEN
24. Frank LATIMORE
25. Michael LEVIN
26. MAEVE
27. MANHATTAN
28. MARSHALL
29. MARY
30. Kate MULGREW
31. NICK
32. PAT
33. RAMONA
34. RIVERSIDE
35. ROGER
36. RYAN'S BAR
37. Upper WEST SIDE

Word-Find 27

```
G B K I E H L S P K K H H A Y
H A N N I B A L N R T E K N K
E R C A A A R Y L I M A F J C
L R X T D R P I A S K W U A U
E O L T M A F F V T S W A C B
N W L A T I M O R E A A A K M
I L E H H I D L D N R T L H U
V V L N Q N B I I Y L S J C L
E R L A U E S C A I N I I N G
L O R M H T K N N M L N D D R
N G D A S S S A I L E D H T E
Y E D E M B R N I T S U J O W
I R W T A O O A D D I S O N J
P C A R G R N B M U L Y V Z H
C L E M O E L A H W I D P D V
```

TV GUIDE WORD-FINDS

1. ADVENTURE
2. AIR travel
3. ANIMALS
4. BICKERING
5. BICYCLES
6. BUSES
7. CAMP out
8. CHALLENGES
9. CHOICES
10. CLUES
11. DESTINATION
12. DETOUR
13. EASIER choice
14. EAT things
15. ELIMINATED
16. FAMILY
17. FAST
18. FINAL leg
19. FLAGS
20. FRIENDS

21. HOST
22. LOST
23. Conserve MONEY
24. OPTIONS
25. PHIL Keoghan
26. PHYSICAL
27. PIT stop
28. REALITY
29. ROAD block
30. ROUTE markers
31. START
32. TASKS
33. TAXIS
34. TEAMS
35. TRAINS
36. TWO people
37. WINNERS
38. Around the
    WORLD

Word-Find 28

```
N Z E T U O R S S D N E I R F
O Q Q A F U P T E E A L U R A
I S Z L O L R T E L V O I P P
T S Y T A A A A I T C A R H O
A Z E L T N N G E O E Y Y S P
N D E S I Q I A S B N S C N W
I K V M Y M M F I I I S C I C
T W I E E S A J X C S S N A B
S L F C N P L F A K L N M R U
E X A H O T S L T E E P I T G
D J S O M Y U W O R L D B E T
K Y T I L A E R S I F T U A T
M H W C H A L L E N G E S A D
B J O E A S I E R G Y K E O T
W G P S E U L C H O S T S A L
```

TV GUIDE WORD-FINDS

TV GUIDE

"The Fugitive"

1. ACCUSED	18. NOT guilty
2. BARRY Morse	19. ODD JOBS
3. BILL Raisch	20. ONE-ARMED MAN
4. CHASE	
5. CONVICTED	21. PHILIP
6. CRIME	22. PURSUIT
7. DAVID JANSSEN	23. RELENTLESS
8. DERAILED	24. RICHARD KIMBLE
9. DOCTOR	
10. DRAMA	25. On the RUN
11. ESCAPE	26. Jacqueline SCOTT
12. EXONERATED	27. SEARCH
13. FRED	28. SUSPENSE
14. GUEST stars	29. TRIAL
15. INNOCENT	30. WIFE
16. NARRATOR	
17. NEW identities	

Word-Find 29

```
S  B  E  F  I  W  E  M  H  S  E  Y  R  Y  P
N  A  M  D  E  M  R  A  E  N  O  I  X  H  I
D  R  I  E  E  D  N  L  E  A  C  Y  W  H  L
A  R  R  L  E  T  O  P  C  H  Z  F  V  R  I
V  Y  C  I  X  B  A  C  A  O  N  A  E  T  H
I  G  N  A  E  C  U  R  T  T  C  L  R  I  P
D  Z  M  R  S  S  D  T  E  O  E  N  N  U  H
J  C  O  E  E  K  A  E  R  N  R  N  A  S  N
A  I  V  D  I  Z  G  H  T  I  O  M  F  R  I
N  K  K  M  D  S  H  L  C  C  A  X  R  U  V
S  G  B  I  L  J  E  X  E  R  I  L  E  P  W
S  L  C  Z  D  S  O  N  D  E  Z  V  L  E  I
E  G  U  E  S  T  T  B  B  C  U  F  N  I  Q
N  A  R  R  A  T  O  R  S  C  O  T  T  O  B
A  F  H  C  R  A  E  S  N  E  P  S  U  S  C
```

TV GUIDE

Top Shows: 1969

1. Green ACRES
2. ADAM 12
3. Let's Make A DEAL
4. The BEVERLY Hillbillies
5. BEWITCHED
6. The BILL Cosby Show
7. BONANZA
8. Daniel BOONE
9. The BRADY Bunch
10. Medical CENTER
11. DRAGNET
12. FAMILY Affair
13. The F.B.I.
14. Hawaii FIVE-O
15. GET Smart
16. That GIRL
17. GUNSMOKE
18. HIGH Chaparral
19. HOGAN'S Heroes
20. I DREAM of Jeannie
21. IRONSIDE
22. JULIA
23. Petticoat JUNCTION
24. LANCER
25. LASSIE
26. LAUGH-IN
27. LOVE, American Style
28. Here's LUCY
29. MANNIX
30. MISSION: Impossible
31. The MOD Squad
32. The Flying NUN
33. Mayberry R.F.D.
34. To ROME with Love
35. The VIRGINIAN
36. WILD Kingdom

Word-Find 30

```
L E L J A S N S B X Q R A S Y
L F O N Z U M F K O O E K X Z
I A J E N A D A M M O C I Q I
B C L U A S J N E V I N V I E
D R A G N E T A X R N A E W K
A E B A O C F I O A D L T B O
L S G W B J T N M H B I P U M
G O Q A U J S I I H E B S Q S
H B V L P I L G O H P F C E N
L R I E D X H R O N G Q T O U
R A D E H C T I W E B U I E G
I D S Y L R E V E B V S A U G
G Y C S V D O M V L S I A L P
R U D L I W F A M I L Y F V H
L R E T N E C R M L A E D A M
```

"Three's a Crowd" Theme

1. YOU
2. AND ME
3. TOGETHER,
4. we're GONNA
5. WEATHER
6. THE ODDS
7. and WIN,
8. LOVERS they
9. can't DIVIDE,
10. MAKING it side
11. by side. TROUBLE
12. MAY BE
13. AROUND us,
14. STANDING our
15. GROUND and
16. we WON'T
17. GIVE IN,
18. SWIMMIN'
19. AGAINST
20. THE TIDE,
21. MAKIN' IT
22. SIDE BY side.
23. LOVE IS
24. FUN,
25. NOW TWO
26. MAKES
27. ONE,
28. WE CAN
29. LAUGH
30. AND CRY,
31. LOVE'S A
32. CRAZY
33. RIDE,
34. WHEN we're
35. side BY SIDE.

TV GUIDE WORD-FINDS

Word-Find 31

```
T L F P J Z D W Y R C D N A V
O V L U R W E C P S Q K H D X
G N I D N A T S W I M M I N Y
E W O N T J P S P N F E L U Z
T F J H M A K I N G D E O O A
H T E L B U O R T I D N V R R
E R Q Q O W E D T I A O E A C
R H T Y T B B E R Z N G S B E
S L Q W Y A H S W N A I A M B
D O O S W T Y E I N S V K N Y
D N I V H G C A D D R E I A A
O D H E E A L M N I E E K A M
E N Y T N I E W I N V B O A W
H G U A L H S A B I O I Y O M
T W P D N U O R G R L G D Y F
```

David Newsom

1. ACTOR
2. "Touched by an ANGEL"
3. Scott BAKULA
4. Beer BOTTLER
5. CATSKILL Actors Theater
6. "CHICAGO HOPE"
7. "CHINA BEACH"
8. Set CONSTRUCTION
9. DELIVERYMAN
10. DOG lover
11. Newspaper EDITOR
12. FENCE installer
13. FILM production
14. "Will & GRACE"
15. GUEST spots
16. "HOMEFRONT"
17. "HOUSE RULES"
18. ITHACA College
19. JESSICA Steen
20. "JUDGING AMY"
21. "Quantum LEAP"
22. MANY JOBS
23. "MELROSE PLACE"
24. NEW YORK
25. "SISTERS"
26. Michael Howard STUDIOS
27. "Suddenly SUSAN"
28. "TALK TO ME"
29. "THE DAYS"
30. WAITER
31. WRITER

Word-Find 32

```
E C A L P E S O R L E M J L B
T O H R Y M A G N I G D U J A
H N P I X S F E N C E J E R L
E S O B C I B E R L Q S L H U
D T E R L A W O I E S C E D K
A R M M F Y G V J I T H A C A
Y U O T O E E O C Y O I P M B
S C T R S R M A H U N N A D R
O T K N Y E I O S O H A E W R
A I L M D W U E H U P B M M E
C O A I E Z R G O D S E R K L
T N T S T U D I O S C A G O T
O O B L L I K S T A C C N M T
R S R E T S I S R E V H P R O
N F S W T L E G N A R Y G M B
```

TV GUIDE WORD-FINDS

"Ironside"

1. ASSISTANTS
2. BARBARA Anderson
3. Elizabeth BAUR
4. BODYGUARD
5. Det. BROWN
6. CARL
7. CASES
8. CHIEF
9. COMMISSIONER
10. Fight CRIME
11. DENNIS
12. DETECTIVES
13. DIANA
14. DON Galloway
15. DRAMA
16. EIGHT seasons
17. GENE Lyons

18. INVESTIGATE
19. JOAN Pringle
20. LAW school
21. MARK
22. Don MITCHELL
23. OFFICE
24. RAYMOND BURR
25. ROBERT IRONSIDE
26. SAN FRANCISCO
27. Johnny SEVEN
28. SOLVE crimes
29. SPECIAL consultant
30. VAN
31. WHEELCHAIR

Word-Find 33

```
B N S K B O Y D S M N W O R B
R A R E N O I S S I M M O C Q
B O U K V A E G P Z N B U B P
I J S R N I B V X E E N O P U
N D R A M A T T L R C D E R E
V D S M N R V C T O Y I R D G
E P T C C F A I E G S U A L E
S Q N A Z R R C U T B N N L E
T U A S L O I A R D E E N E G
I M T E N F R M N V C D S H B
G E S S F D D O E C H C W C C
A Q I O O K M S A E I G H T X
T D S N V Y W G P A E S C I S
E M S B A R B A R A F R C M J
L W A R I A H C L E E H W O E
```

"Love of Life"

1. AUDREY Peters
2. BARROWSVILLE
3. BEANIE
4. Carl BETZ
5. BONNIE Bartlett
6. BRUCE
7. CHARLIE
8. CLAIR
9. COLLIE
10. Richard COOGAN
11. EDWIN Jerome
12. ELLIE
13. FIFTIES
14. Steve GETHERS
15. HAL
16. HILDY Parks
17. MARIE Kenney
18. Jean MCBRIDE
19. Peggy MCCAY
20. MEG

21. MILES
22. MRS. RIVERS
23. Dennis PARNELL
24. PAUL
25. Paul POTTER
26. PROFESSOR
27. Joanna ROOS
28. ROSEHILL
29. SARAH
30. SEVENTIES
31. SISTERS
32. SIXTIES
33. SQUABBLES
34. TOMMY White
35. TUDI Wiggins
36. VANESSA
37. WILL

Word-Find 34

```
Y B A S S E N A V G L W I L L
D K U R E L R H E L B B L Z A
L Z D E X L M M I I O E E Y H
I G R H A I B H V N N I T L K
H X E T L V E B N R R A F Z H
A T Y E X S Q I A A M I E X H
R O S G O W E P M U F R A B Q
A M B R S O O R A T Q O Q L T
S M R C B R S R I U B S M X C
I Y C R H R G E E K L S S M X
S E U B I A S I X T I E S C Q
T C L V R B R I D U T F M C B
E F E L E I L L O C O O G A N
R R X K I E D W I N L R P Y Z
S E I T N E V E S E D P G Q P
```

Athletes on TV: 1984

1. ALAN Trammell
2. ALEKSANDR Dityatin
3. Marcus ALLEN
4. BILL Johnson
5. Larry BIRD
6. Bob CHAMBERLAIN
7. Tiffany COHEN
8. Ben CRENSHAW
9. DALEY Thompson
10. DEAN Osman
11. DEBBIE Armstrong
12. George DICARLO
13. Patrick EWING
14. GEOFF Smith
15. GERTE Waltz
16. GREG Louganis
17. HENRY Tillman
18. Erika HESS
19. JOHN McEnroe
20. Al JOYNER
21. LAFFIT Pincay, Jr.
22. LAURENT Fignon
23. Scott MANNING
24. MARK Messier
25. MARTINA Navratilova
26. MARY LOU Retton
27. Lorraine MOLLER
28. ORLANDO Pizzolato
29. PHIL Mahre
30. PIERRE Quinon
31. PIRMIN Zurbriggen
32. ROSALYN Summers
33. ROWDY Gaines
34. SCOTT Hamilton
35. Michael SPINKS
36. Katarina WITT
37. ZHOU Jihong

Word-Find 35

```
P T Z H O U M C Z J H C B F M
B T Y E L A D W W J O Y N E R
Y I M A R T I N A H N H I M F
A W L Y A Y R N E H O E A O E
P O L L C T D N E J S L L L J
H O Y E I B B E D Y E N R L I
U X W F D E O D A K K P E E A
Y K F G T D L M S N S I B R S
N A R R N Y L A S O R R M F C
L Y E A L A N N U P K M A I O
F G L R M D Y N B R I I H E T
F R I W R D M I Y G E N C H T
O J H S W E R N V I R N K E C
E Y P O I D I G N I W E T S T
G J R R K S F P K W P X G S K
```

Brothers and Sisters

1. ALEX Keaton
2. MALLORY
3. JENNIFER;
4. BETTY Anderson
5. KATHY
6. BUD;
7. CINDY Brady
8. BOBBY
9. GREG
10. PETER
11. MARCIA
12. JAN;
13. DONNY Osmond
14. MARIE;
15. MIKE Seaver
16. CAROL
17. BEN;
18. NICHOLAS

Bradford
19. TOMMY
20. ELIZABETH
21. NANCY
22. SUSAN
23. JOANNIE
24. MARY
25. DAVID;
26. RICHIE
Cunningham
27. JOANIE;
28. SONDRA Huxtable
29. DENISE
30. THEO
31. VANESSA
32. RUDY.

Word-Find 36

```
P B A T V Y E Y K E S E C L N
Y N N O D R E S I I T I Y R R
N A G I H I U Y I N C R V U O
I J V J N Y D U R N K A T H Y
A A M A R C I A R A E M R S X
D A O X N E T K S O M D O O G
B J T Y E E T U D J G N G T L
X O B Y S L S E M V D Y X B R
V I B E U A A S P R Q D Y E I
Y F W B N G L Y A H J N F T C
Y L C P Y R O L L A M I U T H
J Z C B T E H T M Q N C O Y I
H S W H X G C P T N D M I K E
H T E B A Z I L E U M G T L E
D O Y C N A N J B Y W W Y F S
```

1. ADRIENNE Barbeau
2. ARTHUR
3. Conrad BAIN
4. BEA Arthur
5. BERT
6. BILL Macy
7. CAROL
8. CHRIS
9. CONTROVERSY
10. DOMINANT
11. FINDLAY'S
12. FLORIDA
13. FOURTH husband
14. FRIENDS
15. GRANDSON
16. HENRY
17. LIBERAL
18. MAID
19. MARRIED
20. MAUDE
21. MRS. NAUGATUCK
22. NEW YORK
23. NORMAN LEAR
24. OUTSPOKEN
25. PHILLIP
26. POLITICS
27. REALISTIC
28. Esther ROLLE
29. RUE McClanahan
30. SERIOUS issues
31. SIX years
32. SPIN-OFF
33. Appliance STORE
34. VICTORIA
35. VIVIAN
36. WALTER

Word-Find 37

```
N H R X R G R A N D S O N P N
O F O Y U Z F F O N I P S E S
R Y L N H L R M E J J Y W D I
M G L O T N I A B R R Y E N R
A R E E R N E B I N O I R E H
N T S N A I N R E R R T T X C
L C R N C N D H K R O L S T A
E S T E A I S A A U A T H S E
A E P I B U T M T W N L C C B
R R V R Z D G S P H I L L I P
F I D D I F P A I N T B S T V
V O C A R O L A T L R R I I B
A U M U K R U E D U A M U L X
Y S R E V O R T N O C E S O L
F I N D L A Y S C N O K R P F
```

TV GUIDE

"The Jetsons"

1. ANIMATION
2. ASTRO
3. BOSS
4. COGSWELL COGS
5. Digital DIARY
6. EARTH
7. ELROY
8. FAMILY
9. FOLD-UP CAR
10. FUTURE
11. GADGETS
12. GEORGE
13. Miss GYRO
14. HENRY
15. HOMEMAKER
16. JANE
17. JUDY
18. Hydraulic LIFTS
19. LITTLE Dipper School
20. MAID
21. MIDDLE-CLASS
22. MR. SPACELY
23. ROBOT
24. ROSIE
25. SKYPAD Apartments
26. Genius SON
27. Spacely SPROCKETS
28. TALKING dog
29. TEENAGER
30. TV PHONES

Word-Find 38

```
D X T S G B O L I F T S W M I
A G E T Y S M S T E G D A G Y
P S E E R O H G E O R G E N R
Y U N K O A R T C Y W U O O A
K X A C G V C L R H L I S A I
S A G O V P L P E A T I L O D
S M E R F E M N U A E I M T N
F R R P W U R O M D T T V A Q
B O G S B Y T I B T L P X L F
X B G V P H N U L O H O M K G
H O M E M A K E R O S A F I X
C T N F H K C K N E I S B N C
C A S S A L C E L D D I M G E
J L Y O R T S A L V L L X K R
C C J Z Q G Y Q Y Y D U J A A
```

"Moonlighting"

1. ABC
2. Detective AGENCY
3. AGNES
4. ALEXANDER
5. Curtis

   ARMSTRONG
6. Allyce BEASLEY
7. BLUE MOON
8. BRUCE WILLIS
9. Glenn Gordon

   CARON (creator)
10. COMEDY
11. CYBILL

    SHEPHERD

12. DAVID
13. DRAMA
14. EVA MARIE Saint
15. EX-MODEL
16. HERBERT
17. MADDIE
18. PRIVATE EYES
19. QUIRKY
20. ROMANTIC

    tension
21. VIRGINIA
22. Robert WEBBER
23. WISEGUY

Word-Find 39

```
D D A V I D Q Z H C W E B H F
W R E B B E W B A I Z Y Y E K
G E A P D J O R R T C D M R V
N H I M T I O E G N O P A B L
O P F R A N D G E A T P D E N
R E R B A N V G C M R V D R D
T H C I A M A L A O I O I T M
S S P X V E A L U R M S E P A
M L E Q Z A W V G X Q E C A M
R L T G M Q T I E W J N D X F
A I U Y M Z N E S F S G J Y S
Z B Y K R I U Q E E W A U D V
C Y B E A S L E Y Y G C O A H
F C H R E N N O O M E U L B R
T B R U C E W I L L I S Y K Q
```

TV GUIDE

"The Avengers"

1. ACTION
2. ADVENTURE
3. BRITISH
4. CAROL
5. CULT favorite
6. DIANA RIGG
7. ECCENTRIC
8. EMMA PEEL
9. ESPIONAGE
10. Dr. GALE
11. Ian HENDRY
12. HONOR Blackman
13. INGRID Hafner
14. INTELLIGENCE
15. JOHN STEED
16. Dr. KEEL
17. Dr. KING
18. Douglas MUIR
19. NBC
20. ONE-TEN
21. Rhonda PARKER
22. PATRICK MACNEE
23. PRIME TIME
24. Jon ROLLASON
25. SIXTIES
26. Julie STEVENS
27. SUAVE
28. TARA
29. Linda THORSON
30. THRILLER
31. VENUS

```
L A B N G J I W L E E K I N G
F E W R G E R U T N E V D A H
E T E D I R G N I M J Z L N P
N E Y P R T H R I L L E R C Y
A E N Q A L I T W N F S I K M
Y Q S C N M E S O H T R M E I
R J I P A M M S H E T O U V T
E O Y J I M R E V N J L I A U
K H N R D O K E E D C L R U Y
R N P O H H N C W R N A S S Z
A S W T H S C A I Y O S R C O
P T S U N E V U G R I O B O W
L E C N E G I L L E T N I Y L
S E I T X I S U S T C A J A I
Y D I M N E T E N O A B P U D
```

"SpongeBob SquarePants"

1. ADVENTURES
2. Getting ALONG
3. BIKINI Bottom
4. CARTOON
5. CHAOS
6. CHEERFUL
7. CONCH Street
8. DRIVING
9. EUGENE
10. FRED
11. FRIENDS
12. FRYCOOK
13. GARY
14. KRUSTY KRAB
15. MRS. PUFF
16. Grumpy NEIGHBOR
17. NICKELODEON
18. OPTIMISTIC
19. PATCHY
20. PATRICK
21. PEARL
22. PINEAPPLE
23. PIRATE
24. PLANKTON
25. SANDY Cheeks
26. SCOOTER
27. SPONGEBOB
28. SQUIRREL
29. STARFISH
30. Squidward TENTACLES
31. TOM
32. UNDERSEA
33. VILLAGE

Word-Find 41

```
J N P E A R L A R E T O O C S
S O A H C J S K O O C Y R F E
N O T K N A L P A T R I C K L
F T C V N O P T I M I S T I C
A R H D S I E A B T F O E V A
C A Y K R D E D F I M R P Q T
H C S A R S N V O P K U E R N
E S T Q R U I E I L S I O D E
E E I E U L S N I F E B N R T
R U D F L I E T F R H K H I A
F N G A R A R U Y G F H C V L
U Z G E P A P R I K Y S N I O
L E J P N S T E E I R J O N N
K W L F R E N S S L A A C G G
M E N M W X S P O N G E B O B
```

Top Shows: 1992

1. Murphy BROWN
2. CHEERS
3. COACH
4. In Living COLOR
5. The COMMISH
6. COPS
7. Major DAD
8. FAMILY Matters
9. FULL House
10. HEARTS Afire
11. The HEIGHTS
12. Beverly HILLS, 90210
13. HOME Improvement
14. 48 HOURS
15. Doogie HOWSER, M.D.
16. KNOTS Landing
17. L.A. LAW
18. Quantum LEAP
19. LIFE Goes On
20. MAD About You
21. MARTIN
22. 60 MINUTES
23. Empty NEST
24. NORTHERN Exposure
25. PICKET Fences
26. Melrose PLACE
27. ROC
28. ROSEANNE
29. SEINFELD
30. Evening SHADE
31. The SIMPSONS
32. SISTERS
33. WINGS
34. Designing WOMEN
35. The Wonder YEARS

Word-Find 42

```
H S R U O H S G K G Y V S D N
E Y C J R R E F I L G T N V R
I J O S E T U N I M O B O I E
G J P T C O E M H N D L S N H
H Y S J Q O A P K I C A P E T
T I L L U F A E S T L N M M R
S R A E Y D K C R R S L I O O
W H D C Z R L B H A E E S W N
A K A H O W S E R M D E N V P
L I D D N M A U F I A X H L W
A F R W E R M W I N G S A C L
L E O E T I Z I N P I C K E T
C R L S M B R E S A E E A X N
B N O W B O Z N C H Y P S Y C
X Z C T C C H H E J V I K Y R
```

"Dynasty" Dynasty?

1. ABC tried
2. to COPY
3. the SUCCESS
4. OF ITS
5. HIT
6. SOAP
7. "DYNASTY"
8. WITH the
9. SPIN-OFF
10. "The COLBYS,"
11. WHICH
12. DEBUTED
13. in NINETEEN
14. EIGHTY-
15. FIVE.
16. EMMA
17. SAMMS,
18. WHO HAD
19. TAKEN
20. OVER the
21. ROLE of
22. FALLON from
23. PAMELA Sue
24. MARTIN
25. the YEAR
26. BEFORE,
27. HEADED up
28. the CAST,
29. ALONG
30. with MOVIE
31. VETERANS
32. BARBARA
33. STANWYCK,
34. CHARLTON
35. HESTON, and
36. KATHERINE
37. ROSS.
38. STEPHANIE
39. BEECHAM
40. PLAYED
41. Heston's WIFE,
42. SABLE.

Word-Find 43

```
E I N A H P E T S S O R X P E
N I A M R Z S N S P L A Y E D
I E S W O O A C D E B U T E D
R N N S L R V E B Y B I S C U
E K I D E D A E H A H S A A V
H B N T W C H A R L T O N S Y
T Y E A R F C B W A L H Y T B
A V T E I A A U N H R C D I E
K M E V C R M W S P I N O F F
D G E I A H Y E A Y O C T O O
A E N X G C A M T L B A H W R
H I L O K H E M L D K L I C E
O V R B L L T A H E S T O N F
H O U C A A F Y N F H P J C I
W M P A O S M M A S Y I Y T W
```

Food Channels

1. ARNOLD'S Drive-In
2. The BAGEL
3. The Pizza BARN
4. BOCELLI'S
5. The Lunch BOX
6. The BRICK
7. The BURGER Palace
8. CARMEN'S
9. CASA Tacos
10. DANNY'S Place
11. The New York DELI
12. The DEN
13. DINO'S
14. GOODIE Goodie
15. The HUB
16. Café JACQUES
17. JUNCTION Café
18. The Krusty KRAB
19. LA SCALA
20. LIAISONS
21. MAGOO'S
22. Café MAISON
23. The MAX
24. MCGINTY'S
25. MONK'S Café
26. MORY'S
27. Café NERVOSA
28. NICKY St. Hubbin's
29. O'NEILL'S
30. O'PHELAN'S
31. The PEACH Pit
32. Central PERK
33. PETRONIS
34. PIZZA Bowl
35. POP'S Joint
36. POTATO Palace
37. The QUAKE
38. ROB'S
39. SALINGER'S
40. The SHACK
41. TONY Packo's
42. WILLIE'S Chili
43. Charlie WONG'S

Word-Find 44

```
W K X N S Y T N I G C M A X S
X R P O C A R M E N S C B B J
O E B I B S L H W S K N O M W
T P E T R O N I S S E R C F M
A L A C S A L O N L D M E F O
T T O N Y L B A S G A E L I R
O N N U S A L O Z I E J L E Y
P S E J R E N I S Z A R I I S
S P R N H I I O E C I I S D E
P O V P D R N L Q N W P L O K
S P O A D I P U L E O O L O A
R H S G C E E I E I N K N G U
F A A K A S N V G R W C R G Q
C J Y C F M U D A N N Y S A S
B U H U K C I R B U R G E R B
```

Dan Curtis

1. AUGUST birthday
2. "A Darkness at BLAISEDON"
3. BRIDGEPORT, CT
4. "BURNT Offerings"
5. CONNECTICUT
6. "CURSE of the Black Widow"
7. DIRECTOR
8. "The Picture of DORIAN GRAY"
9. "DRACULA"
10. "DR. JEKYLL and Mr. Hyde"
11. "EXPRESS to Terror"
12. "The GREAT Ice Rip-Off"
13. "INTRUDERS"
14. "JOHNNY RYAN"
15. "The KANSAS CITY Massacre"
16. "The Love LETTER"
17. "The NIGHT STALKER"
18. PRODUCER
19. "War and REMEM-BRANCE"
20. "Dark SHADOWS"
21. "SUPERTRAIN"
22. "The Norliss TAPES"
23. "Me and THE KID"
24. "TRILOGY of Terror"
25. "The WINDS of War"
26. "Scream of the WOLF"
27. WRITER

Word-Find 45

```
R  R  S  T  F  Y  T  S  U  G  U  A  O  E  B
L  E  T  T  E  R  W  P  J  W  M  H  X  E  R
S  K  M  F  L  O  W  T  R  S  I  P  B  Y  I
S  L  N  E  D  R  H  T  U  O  R  N  T  B  D
S  A  F  A  M  E  O  P  A  E  D  I  D  B  G
R  T  H  Y  K  B  E  T  S  P  C  U  L  S  E
E  S  B  I  A  R  R  S  C  S  E  A  C  J  P
D  T  D  W  T  R  C  A  A  E  I  S  N  E  O
U  H  R  R  C  S  G  S  N  S  R  Z  R  L  R
R  G  A  I  C  O  N  N  E  C  T  I  C  U  T
T  I  C  T  Z  A  B  D  A  J  E  G  D  B  C
N  N  U  E  K  U  O  T  R  I  L  O  G  Y  T
I  Z  L  R  R  N  Y  T  A  E  R  G  G  F  J
V  S  A  N  A  Y  R  Y  N  N  H  O  J  M  Q
U  O  T  A  B  L  L  Y  K  E  J  R  D  M  X
```

"Search for Tomorrow"

1. ABIGAIL Kellogg
2. ARTHUR
3. BESS Johnson
4. CLIFF
5. Dr. COLLINS
6. DOUG
7. DR. VINCENTE
8. EUNICE
9. GEORGE
10. Lee GRANT
11. Larry HAINES
12. HAZEL
13. HENDERSON Hospital
14. IRENE
15. JANET
16. JOANNE
17. JOHNNY
18. KEITH
19. LEIGH Lassen
20. Lynn LORING
21. MARGE
22. MARY Stuart
23. MELBA Rae
24. NATHAN
25. Terry O'SULLIVAN
26. PATTI
27. ROBERT Mandan
28. ROSE
29. SAM
30. SCOTT
31. STEPHANIE
32. STUART
33. SUZI
34. TINA Sloan
35. TONY
36. VICTOR

Word-Find 46

```
E T N E C N I V R D Y C O R S
W A B I G A I L G G N I R O L
E U E N P L Z E D A N I W B B
G X K A O N O T V Y H T I E K
C X T H C R R I R A O Y S R W
N T N P G A L A I I J S F T T
I N F E U L M N R R O T C I V
Z X O T U X E E N S U S F H M
U J S S Y S N T I N A H G M E
S L O Z R E B N J I J I T A L
L E N A M E U T C L E A L R B
Y Z V M N D D N T L U S N G A
N A T H A N O N I O I V S E I
O H U R O S E U E C C F B Y T
T Y E L T N A R G H E S F H U
```

TV GUIDE

"Naked City"

1. ACTION
2. Sgt. ARCARO
3. Harry BELLAVER
4. CRIME drama
5. DETECTIVES
6. "EIGHT MILLION stories"
7. Det. FLINT
8. James FRANCISCUS
9. Paul FREES
10. GUEST STARS
11. Det. HALLORAN
12. Human INTEREST
13. JANET
14. LIBBY
15. LOCATION
16. John MCINTIRE
17. Horace MCMAHON
18. Lt. MULDOON
19. NANCY Malone
20. NARRATOR
21. NEW YORK
22. Lt. PARKER
23. PAUL Burke
24. POLICE
25. 65th PRECINCT
26. PRIME TIME
27. REALISM
28. STREETS
29. SUSPENSE
30. SUZANNE Storrs
31. TAG LINE

TV GUIDE WORD-FINDS

```
D R C Y C N A N P A R K E R A
S B T R E O K R E L B C X A C
T E I T S S E R E N I L G A T
E M R H R V N M O L N M X C I
E I O I A F Q E O Y U A N M O
R R G L T L A P P L W I Z A N
T N L H S N L R D S C E I U U
S E O N T S I O C E U L N B S
B N C N S M O C R A U S T H J
F O A T E N I P M A R R E Y K
J H T T U Z F L P I N O R B T
A A I L G R E A L I S M E B N
N M O D E T E C T I V E S I I
E C N E N A R R A T O R T L L
T M S Q R S U C S I C N A R F
```

Agnes Nixon

1. **ABC**
2. **AGGIE (nickname)**
3. **"ANOTHER WORLD"**
4. **CBS**
5. **CHICAGO**
6. **"All My CHILDREN"**
7. **CONSULTANT**
8. **CREATIVE**
9. **DAYTIME television**
10. **DECEMBER birthday**
11. **Agnes ECKHARDT Nixon**
12. **EPISODES**
13. **"The GUIDING LIGHT"**
14. **"LOVING"**
15. **NBC**
16. **NEW YORK**
17. **NORTH-WESTERN Univ.**
18. **"ONE LIFE to Live"**
19. **PIONEER**
20. **ROBERT Nixon**
21. **ROMANCE**
22. **"SEARCH for Tomorrow"**
23. **SERIAL dramas**
24. **SOAP OPERAS**
25. **STORYTELLING**
26. **"THE CITY"**
27. **"As the WORLD TURNS"**
28. **Head WRITER**

```
D E W O R L D T U R N S K S T
N R E T S E W H T R O N R N S
B L A I S S V G T R E B O R Q
C X A R T C H I C A G O Y A O
W P J I O D D L T C I A W N E
N R G C R A L G O A S G E O C
C E I X Y E P N L E E L N T N
J K R T T E S I I G I R D H A
T Q I D E U P D O F N R C E M
H M S T L R Z I E N A I I R O
E O E T L I G U S H E G V W R
C K A T I E H G K O G E S O T
I N R W N S K C B A D B R R L
T S C F G R E B M E C E D L E
Y W H S O A P O P E R A S D I
```

TV GUIDE

"Hee Haw"

1. Roy ACUFF
2. ARCHIE Campbell
3. John AYLESWORTH
4. BARBI BENTON
5. CATHY Baker
6. DON Harron
7. DUB Taylor
8. GAILARD Sartain
9. GEORGE Lindsey
10. GRANDPA JONES
11. GUNILLA Hutton
12. IRLENE Mandrell
13. JACKIE Phelps
14. JOHN HENRY Faulk
15. JUNIOR Samples
16. KENNY Price
17. LINDA Thompson
18. LISA Todd
19. LULU Roman
20. MARIANNE Gordon
21. MINNIE PEARL
22. MISTY Rowe
23. Rev. Grady NUTT
24. Buck OWENS
25. RONI Stoneman
26. ROY CLARK
27. SHEB Wooley
28. SLIM Pickens
29. STRINGBEAN
30. Gordie TAPP
31. Buck TRENT
32. VICTORIA Hallman
33. Jonathan WINTERS

Word-Find 49

```
S E N O J A P D N A R G B P E
T T O W O J X S L I M E I P U
N W T B Y O H L E I H C R A A
E A N U S H I K N S D X L T J
R C E D N N T N G V S O E U W
T U B B U H I A G A Y N N E K
P F I G G E D R C E I I E R G
K F B D P N B L D M O L D W K
P R R E I R I H A R C R A S O
L U A L F Y O R D G I V G R P
U R B L T V I C T O R I A E D
L I I S C A Y L E S W O R T H
U S I T N Y W V S S X B D N G
A M B N U T O J E J A C K I E
G I E X I N O R X F F H C W Y
```

TV
GUIDE

"Felicity"

1. AMANDA Foreman
2. AMY JO Johnson
3. Amy AQUINO
4. BEN
5. CAROL
6. Mr. COVINGTON
7. ELENA
8. Donald FAISON
9. Jennifer GARNER
10. Ian GOMEZ
11. GREG Grunberg
12. GUY
13. HANNAH
14. JAVIER
15. JULIE
16. Jane KACZMAREK
17. KERI Russell
18. Brian KLUGMAN
19. MAGGIE
20. Dr. MCGRATH
21. MEGAN
22. MOLLY
23. NOEL
24. Dr. PAVONE
25. Teri POLO
26. Sarah-Jane POTTS
27. PROFESSOR Sherman
28. RICHARD
29. John RITTER
30. ROBERT Patrick Benedict
31. SALLY Kirkland
32. Chris SARANDON
33. SCOTT Foley
34. SEAN
35. Scott SPEEDMAN
36. TANGI Miller
37. TRACY

Word-Find 50

```
R P A V O N E L Z Q U Y A E I
H I O K E R A M Z C A K Q P G
V J C T C Z R M O L L Y U H N
E E U H T A B M D V B U I T A
R R C L A S R C N E U D N A T
R E T T I R R O S S E F O R P
J I N O D E D V L O K P A G S
M V V R Y N V I O L O C S C A
H A N N A H G N U O Y J O M B
T J G R E G O G O P A T Y N S
R O A G I S M T S M T J L U F
E S K R I A E O A O O Q L N G
B V E A N E Z N A G E M A N M
O K F K H F D L E O N E S J D
R E L E N A F N Q B S Z D L X
```

"Laverne & Shirley"

1. ABC	17. David L. LANDER
2. APARTMENT	18. LOS ANGELES
3. Mrs. BABISH	19. Michael MCKEAN
4. BETTY Garrett	20. Eddie MEKKA
5. BLUE-COLLAR	21. MILWAUKEE
6. BOO-BOO KITTY	22. NOSTALGIA
7. BOTTLE CAPS	23. PENNY Marshall
8. BOWLING	24. PHIL Foster
9. CARMINE	25. RHONDA
10. CINDY Williams	26. ROOMMATES
11. FRANK	27. SEVEN-YEAR run
12. Best FRIENDS	28. SHIRLEY
13. "HAPPY DAYS"	29. SHOTZ Brewery
14. LAVERNE	30. SPIN-OFF
15. LENNY	31. SQUIGGY
16. LESLIE Easterbrook	32. THEME SONG

Word-Find 51

```
Y Y N N E P L E S L I E Q K E
U T N F R A N K F F O N I P S
L U T N S R A E Y N E V E S T
L F S I E S Y A D Y P P A H Y
L L P V K L A P A R T M E N T
D R A L L O C E U L B M A E T
M L C N O R O O C Y E E R N E
G I E B D S Y B G S K N O I B
U U L O Y E A F O C Q S O M A
R S T W Y G R N M O T H M R B
L H T L A I G C G A B I M A I
I O O I E U I I L E B R A C S
H T B N Q N K G U I L L T D H
P Z D G D V I E K Q W E E L S
S S J Y C A K K E M S Y S M O
```

TV GUIDE

"Dark Shadows"

1. ANGELIQUE
2. BARNABAS
3. BLACKMAIL
4. CAROLYN
5. COAST
6. COLLINSPORT, ME
7. COLLINWOOD
8. CURSE
9. DAN CURTIS (creator)
10. ESTATE
11. Collins FAMILY
12. FLORA
13. Jonathan FRID
14. GHOST
15. GHOUL
16. GOTHIC soap opera
17. GOVERNESS
18. GRAYSON Hall
19. HEIRESS
20. Alexandra ISLES
21. JEREMIAH
22. JOEL Crothers
23. JOSETTE
24. JULIA
25. LARA Parker
26. MAINE
27. NANCY Barrett
28. NATALIE
29. NATHAN
30. VAMPIRE
31. VICTORIA
32. Fishing VILLAGE
33. WEREWOLF
34. WITCH

Word-Find 52

```
U L U G E G P N A H T A N V W
B I N O H N O A I L U J A E I
E A C B E O I T C D R M R G T
S M R O E U U A H I P E H U C
T K T N A T Q L M I W I G C H
A C S R A S T I R O C O N S D
T A O V O B T E L N V L Y I O
E L H X L P A F S E E N L T E
F B G O L F S S R O G A O R M
V I L L A G E N J I J N R U E
H A I M E R E J I A D C A C S
Q Q I T I S Z X R L W Y C N R
G L H E S X F A I S L E S A U
Y P H N C O L L I N W O O D C
N O S Y A R G A I R O T C I V
```

"Monk" Theme

1. IT'S a jungle
2. out THERE.
3. DISORDER and
4. CONFUSION
5. EVERYWHERE.
6. No ONE
7. SEEMS to
8. CARE. Well
9. I DO.
10. HEY WHO'S in
11. CHARGE here?
12. It's a JUNGLE
13. OUT there.
14. POISON in
15. THE VERY air
16. we BREATHE.
17. Do you KNOW
18. WHAT'S in
19. the WATER
20. THAT you
21. DRINK?
22. WELL I do,
23. AND it's
24. AMAZING.
25. PEOPLE think
26. I'm CRAZY,
27. 'CAUSE I
28. WORRY all
29. the TIME.
30. If you PAID
31. ATTENTION, you'd
32. be WORRIED too.
33. You BETTER
34. PAY attention
35. or this WORLD
36. we LOVE so
37. MUCH might
38. JUST kill you.
39. I COULD be
40. WRONG now,
41. BUT I don't
42. THINK so.

Word-Find 53

```
Q T H E R E T A W P Y K O O R
P S C C R E M U A D R N M E Z
J U U C R A Z Y R Y E S T L D
U J M D Z Z C I R V V T H P L
D P O I S O N R E W E A I O F
N M N S G K O R I B H H N E V
A G S O H W Y E H E T W K P H
D T O R C W E W H I S J N W W
K E T D H H R T W D L U O C I
H J I E S O A F I O Z N A U R
L A R R N E R R E L R G N C T
P E D G R T E M G E L L W E I
I T U B S O I M F E V E D O S
B J T A H T W O S K N O W G J
C O N F U S I O N V U V L L U
```

TV GUIDE WORD-FINDS

"Summerland"

1. AUNT	19. Jesse
2. AVA	MCCARTNEY
3. BEACH	20. MERRIN Dungey
4. BOUTIQUE	21. NEPHEWS
5. BRADIN	22. NICK Benson
6. BUSINESS	23. NIECE
7. CALIFORNIA	24. NIKKI
8. DERRICK	25. RYAN Kwanten
9. DRAMA	26. SHAWN Christian
10. ERICA	27. SURFING
11. FAMILY	28. SUSANNAH
12. FASHION designer	29. TAYLOR Cole
13. Father FIGURE	30. TEENS
14. FRIENDS	31. THREE children
15. JAY	32. TRANSITION
16. JOHNNY	33. WB NETWORK
17. KAY Panabaker	
18. Lori LOUGHLIN	

Word-Find 54

```
H Q Z I K K I N Y N N H O J U
H A N N A S U S T I X I J I N
F R I E N D S Z L H T Q E O C
W W E R P D R H N R R F T C R
B O R I X H G Y W M Z E Z D E
N B U C B U E Y A K E M E D J
E O G A O U R W H N C R E S S
T N I L U G S I S C D R R R P
W V F T T N B I A S R B Y I G
O C A L I F O R N I A W L N N
R X P C Q S T I C E D P I T I
K C K A U N N K H R S D M N F
E J P Y E M J A A S A S A U R
M T A Y L O R M R R A V F A U
O J W J H C A E B T Z F A K S
```

Allan Burns

1. Commercial ARTIST
2. BALTIMORE
3. BUCK Henry
4. "The BULLWINKLE Show"
5. CARTOONIST
6. EMMY Awards
7. "The Duck FACTORY"
8. Feature FILMS
9. "Fractured FLICKERS"
10. "GET SMART"
11. GREETING cards
12. "JUST THE WAY You Are"
13. LOS ANGELES
14. "LOU GRANT"
15. "Eisenhower & LUTZ"
16. MARYLAND
17. "MARY TYLER MOORE"
18. MAY birthday
19. MEL BROOKS
20. "The MUNSTERS"
21. "MY MOTHER the Car"
22. University of OREGON
23. OSCAR nomination
24. "RHODA"
25. "ROCKY and His Friends"
26. SCREENPLAYS
27. Grant TINKER
28. Jay WARD
29. WRITERS GUILD Award

Word-Find 55

```
M Y C S R E T S N U M E F Y G
O A F A C T O R Y H H W K M Y
A R R L R M A R Y L A N D M A
D T E Y D T S K O O R B L E M
O P R G T W O S D M G G S B Y
H L Y A O Y A O Z R N Z Y U M
R G O L M N L S N I A E A L O
D L I U G S R E T I R W L L T
R C U E G E T E R O S A P W H
A E L T K R E E M M R T N I E
C E K C Z R A I G T O K E N R
S W I N G E T N I K C O E K O
O L X F I L M S T U K D R L O
F A V M A T T K B D Y R C E S
O G D B G Y A W E H T T S U J
```

"The Waltons"

1. BEN
2. Rev. BUCHANAN
3. CINDY
4. CORABETH
5. ELIZABETH
6. Miss EMILY
7. ERIN
8. ESTHER
9. FLOSSIE
10. Rev. FORDWICK
11. IKE
12. JASON
13. J.D. PICKETT
14. JEFFREY
15. JIM BOB
16. JOHN BOY
17. JOHN CURTIS
18. JOHN, SR.
19. JONSEY
20. Miss MAMIE
21. Rev. MARSHALL
22. MARY ELLEN
23. MAUDE
24. NARRATOR
25. OLIVIA
26. ROSEMARY
27. SERENA
28. SHERIFF Bridges
29. TONI
30. VERDIE
31. Dr. WILLARD
32. YANCY
33. ZEB

Word-Find 56

```
T V N E B K E Y H D I V W J Y
J L V K K C S C T J F O A Z I
M O O E M I Q B E I S S O L F
A A H C R W L F B J O N S E Y
R F U N O D F N A N A H C U B
S Y F D B R I Z Z D I R W K M
H I J I E O A E I E T P I S T
A G T Y R F Y B L T I E L D Y
L M A R Y E L L E N S M L R L
L T I V U R H K G T R N A H I
Y D V C L C C S H S H M R M M
C J I I I I N E N R E K D P E
N N L N P X R H A S E R E N A
A Z O D U I O R O T A R R A N
Y T J Y N J Z R I J I M B O B
```

TV GUIDE WORD-FINDS

1. ALMOST
2. a DECADE
3. AFTER they
4. had APPEARED
5. TOGETHER on
6. the SERIES
7. "MISSION:
8. IMPOSSIBLE,"
9. MARTIN
10. LANDAU and
11. his THEN-WIFE
12. BARBARA
13. BAIN
14. COSTARRED in
15. the SCI-FI
16. CULT favorite
17. "SPACE: 1999."
18. They PLAYED
19. COMMANDER
20. John KOENIG
21. AND DR.
22. Helena RUSSELL,
23. HELMING a
24. RESEARCH
25. COLONY,
26. MOONBASE
27. ALPHA.
28. The SHOW
29. TOTALED
30. FORTY-EIGHT
31. EPISODES,
32. ENDING its
33. RUN IN
34. NINETEEN
35. SEVENTY-EIGHT.

TV GUIDE WORD-FINDS

Word-Find 57

```
C T H E N W I F E H H T N C Y
O N H B N Y G Y D H H O B O E
L D I G N I D N E G I U C M P
O L E T I E L B I S S O P M I
N K E L R E K E S M S E T A S
Y I O S A A Y I A T L O O N O
H F N E S T M T A N G E R D D
C I C E N U O R R E D E H E E
R C L E T I R T T O T D A R S
A S V L W E G H O F F H R L E
E E U O D D E R A E P P A E R
S C H B E R E N O L P N B C I
E S A B N O O M A F D U R A E
R I D E C A D E Y A L P A P S
N T S O M L A R U N I N B S Q
```

TV GUIDE

Top Shows: 2000

1. ALLY McBeal
2. Judging AMY
3. ANGEL
4. BECKER
5. BOSTON Public
6. CHARMED
7. COPS
8. Yes, DEAR
9. DHARMA & Greg
10. The DISTRICT
11. FELICITY
12. FRASIER
13. FRIENDS
14. Gilmore GIRLS
15. 7th HEAVEN
16. JAG
17. KING of Queens

18. LAW & Order
19. That's LIFE
20. MOESHA
21. NASH Bridges
22. NIKKI
23. Normal, OHIO
24. ROSWELL
25. The SIMPSONS
26. SPIN City
27. THAT '70s Show
28. THIRD Watch
29. TITUS
30. The WEST Wing
31. WILL & Grace
32. The X FILES

Word-Find 58

```
E L N L G B I Z A T V T T Y D
G B E I A R O K R R A E D R P
R T R G P W E S T H O O C T G
Y L L A N S V L T K K I K O P
S S L D H A R M A O N I X D S
F R I E N D S T R G N J F N Z
O H W M W T Z Z T G G W I E K
P O S R P S Y P C G I K L F B
K N I A O S O K I F K R E I S
J E V H N Q O R R I E L S L P
S V G C O G E N T I I B D E O
M A M Y G K N U S C A O R B C
J E B V C M J A I H A R I A A
A H S E O M R T D Y Q Z H R N
O I B J L F Y H S U T I T E C
```

TV GUIDE WORD-FINDS

"WKRP in Cincinnati"

1. ANDY
2. BAILEY
3. Carol BRUCE
4. Mr. CARLSON
5. CBS
6. CINCINNATI
7. DR. JOHNNY FEVER
8. FRANK Bonner
9. GARY Sandy
10. HERB
11. Howard HESSEMAN
12. JENNIFER
13. Disc JOCKEYS
14. Gordon JUMP
15. LES NESSMAN

16. LONI Anderson
17. MAMA Carlson
18. Station MANAGER
19. PROGRAM director
20. RADIO station
21. Tim REID
22. REPORTER
23. SALES manager
24. Richard SANDERS
25. SECRETARY
26. SITCOM
27. Jan SMITHERS
28. VENUS FLYTRAP
29. Hugh WILSON (creator)

Word-Find 59

```
P L E S N E S S M A N G R O V
V F C R C A T I R B R E H R H
D Z U U U W P T R E G A N A M
B R R E I D Q C P X H J T D V
M B J L J V J O J N N T C I O
H A S O Z E R M O U A P I O H
I O R W H T N S K Y M Q N M B
N G Y G E N L N R F E P C S S
F A D R O R N A I U S B I R N
S R N P A R T Y L F S U N E V
I Y A C Y E P S F Z E Z N D L
R N H N R Y C F E E H R A N D
X J O C K E Y S U L V M T A S
M Y E L I A B Y U L A E I S F
A S W N F L Q K G M Q S R I S
```

Macdonald Carey

1. ACTOR
2. AUTO-BIOGRAPHY
3. BEVERLY HILLS
4. "BRANDED"
5. BROADWAY
6. CHARM
7. "DAYS of Our Lives"
8. "DR. CHRISTIAN"
9. "DREAM Girl"
10. EMMY Awards
11. EVERYMAN appeal
12. FILMS
13. "The Great GATSBY"
14. Alfred HITCHCOCK
15. HOLLYWOOD
16. Dr. Tom HORTON, SR.
17. University of IOWA
18. LEADING MAN
19. "LOCK UP"
20. MAGNETISM
21. MARCH birthday
22. NBC
23. POETRY
24. RADIO
25. "The REBELS"
26. "ROOTS"
27. "SHADOW of a Doubt"
28. SIOUX CITY, Iowa
29. SIX children
30. SOAP OPERA Hall of Fame
31. STAGE
32. VOICE-OVER

TV GUIDE WORD-FINDS

Word-Find 60

```
B R O A D W A Y H C M A E R D
Y Z S D C K S I B A Y M Y N O
B S O N R T T D R R M Z A C S
S I W L O C O C S Y A M B T B
T O P O H T H R L I G N A P V
A U R C D M R R L N X G D O S
G X O K O A V O I C E O V E R
U C Y U O G H D H S E D S T D
K I S P W N A S Y R T L A R W
C T C M Y E Z S L Q E I K Y M
H Y E W L T B M R B L K A E S
A W O I L I E V E R Y M A N Y
R A D I O S F R V Z Z H K E D
M G Y T H M A R E P O P A O S
Y H P A R G O I B O T U A B U
```

TV GUIDE WORD-FINDS

"Promised Land" Voice-Over

1. My NAME
2. is RUSSELL
3. GREENE.
4. MAYBE you've
5. PASSED me and
6. my FAMILY out
7. on the HIGHWAY.
8. Maybe you WERE
9. DRIVING some
10. fancy SPORTS
11. CAR or an
12. OLD beat-up
13. FOUR-
14. DOOR. Or maybe
15. YOU'VE had some
16. HARD times
17. LIKE us and
18. you're OUT on
19. the ROAD
20. with YOUR
21. HOUSE
22. HITCHED up
23. BEHIND ya
24. and AMERICA
25. the BEAUTIFUL
26. up AHEAD.
27. BUT whoever
28. you ARE,
29. you be SURE
30. to GIVE
31. us a WAVE
32. NEXT time you
33. DRIVE by,
34. 'CAUSE we're
35. your NEIGHBORS.
36. We're ALL ON
37. the road
   TOGETHER.

Word-Find 61

```
P G W D R A H H S E H Q E Y T
X R X C C F H R Y V N H B Y R
Y E N A O D O E F A C B Y N O
D E R U A B S T A W W K A K D
T N R O H U N R C D X H M A X
W E I G O E D R I V I N G C S
B X I H X D Y S T R O P S I Y
R E H T E G O T H B X Y U R H
N D A R R B N I A L L O N E Q
J Y O U V E T A J I D E U M P
W E O S T C C U M K R R O A D
F Y R S H I I A B E I U S X Q
G I V E P H F O U Q V S E T J
G K D L W S G U L S E D F U H
V S U L S G V W L D E R A O V
```

"The Thorn Birds"

1. ANNE
2. AUSTRALIA
3. BARBARA Stanwyck
4. BARRY Corbin
5. BRYAN Brown
6. Richard CHAMBERLAIN
7. CHRISTOPHER Plummer
8. DANE
9. EARL Holliman
10. Financial EMPIRE
11. EPIC miniseries
12. FIONA
13. FORBIDDEN LOVE
14. FRANK
15. HARRY
16. Ken HOWARD
17. JEAN Simmons
18. JUSTINE
19. LUDDIE
20. LUKE
21. MARY
22. MEGGIE
23. OUTBACK
24. PADDY
25. PHILIP Anglim
26. PIPER Laurie
27. Catholic PRIEST
28. RACHEL Ward
29. RAINER
30. RALPH
31. RICHARD Kiley
32. STEPHANIE Faracy
33. SYDNEY Penny
34. Richard VENTURE
35. VITTORIO
36. Mare WINNINGHAM

Word-Find 62

```
R E P I P I L I H P A N X E J
G M E G G I E L K B R F M K K
J N A E J M B N W A A I F U I
O S T E P H A N I E B O E L O
C I G I P R Q L N D R N I S W
K H R L F I A K N B A A D Y T
L E A O E R C I I Q B A D D L
D R T M T A I D N E N H U N Q
J Q N S B T D C G E G O L E H
U J U T B E I E H Y R W E Y L
S A U R N H R V A A R A N R J
T O Y L A R F L M R R R N A H
I A O R L E H C A R L D A M C
N V R E H P O T S I R H C B X
E Y D D A P E R U T N E V G A
```

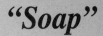

"Soap"

1. ARTHUR Peterson
2. BENSON
3. BILLY
4. BURT
5. BUTLER
6. John BYNER
7. CARLOS
8. CHESTER
9. CHUCK/BOB
10. CORINNE
11. Billy CRYSTAL
12. Cathryn DAMON
13. DANNY
14. DIANA Canova
15. Det. DONAHUE
16. DONNELLY Rhodes
17. DUTCH
18. EUNICE
19. Robert GUILLAUME
20. Katherine HELMOND
21. JAY Johnson
22. JESSICA
23. JIMMY Baio
24. JODIE
25. The MAJOR
26. Robert MANDAN
27. MARY
28. Richard MULLIGAN
29. Jennifer SALT
30. Gregory SIERRA
31. THE CAMPBELLS
32. THE TATES
33. Father TIMOTHY
34. VENTRILOQUIST
35. Sal VISCUSO
36. Ted WASS

Word-Find 63

```
D L L A T S Y R C J L X J D O
G D C O R I N N E M A N D A N
T V A E J O S S V T S S O M Y
B S N Q S W S E I I S S N O K
S Y I N Q I J M U E S E A N T
B H E U C R O U T N C C H W E
I B C A Q T E A N A I D U C I
L M H T H O T L R L L C E S D
L R U Y U E L L T T D D E I O
Y U C L H D O I R U A N T E J
Y H K T L S X U R N B O L R L
M T B A U I B G N T J M A R Y
M R O J A M G Y G M N L S A A
I A B T H E C A M P B E L L S
J W H Y L L E N N O D H V A T
```

TV GUIDE

Stirling Silliphant

1. **ADVENTURE novels**
2. **ADVERTISING executive**
3. **Wrote 50+ BOOKS**
4. **"CHARLY"**
5. **DETROIT**
6. **DISNEY**
7. **"FLY AWAY HOME"**
8. **GOLDEN Globe**
9. **"Alfred HITCHCOCK Presents"**
10. **"The Towering INFERNO"**
11. **JANUARY birthday**
12. **"LONGSTREET"**
13. **"MR. LUCKY"**
14. **"NAKED CITY"**
15. **"NIGHTFALL"**
16. **"PEARL"**
17. **"PERRY MASON"**
18. **Edgar Allan POE AWARD**
19. **"The POSEIDON Adventure"**
20. **PRODUCER**
21. **PROLIFIC**
22. **"RAWHIDE"**
23. **"ROUTE 66"**
24. **"SUSPICION"**
25. **"The SWARM"**
26. **USC**
27. **WRITER**
28. **"ZANE GREY Theater"**

Word-Find 64

```
D A Y U J A N U A R Y L P J S
A S C L N E D L O G R R E U W
D W I S R I X V C A O O S Y R
V A F L U A R O E D G P U Y I
E R I R P P H P U N I Z D T T
R M L A K C O C H C T I H I E
T R O W O U E S I E S U O C R
I L R H U R D O E N K R R D Q
S U P I Y Y N R E I T N Z E Y
I C H D V A T Y A E D D K K F
N K N E A S W B D W O O T A U
G Y E R G E N A Z T A W N N T
H A R N O S A M Y R R E P T H
F Z O N R E F N I L B O O K S
L L A F T H G I N M F I V P G
```

1. SAM Benedict
2. SANFORD AND SON
3. SARA
4. SATURDAY Night Live
5. SAVED BY the Bell
6. SCRUBS
7. SEA HUNT
8. SEAQUEST DSV
9. SECOND CITY TV
10. SECRET Agent
11. SEINFELD
12. SHA NA NA
13. SHASTA McNasty
14. SHE'S the Sheriff
15. SHINDIG
16. SILVER Spoons
17. SISTER KATE
18. SISTERS
19. SKY KING
20. SLEDGE HAMMER!
21. SOAP
22. SOLID GOLD
23. SOUTH PARK
24. SPACE: 1999
25. SPIN CITY
26. SQUARE Pegs
27. STAR SEARCH
28. STAR TREK
29. ST. ELSEWHERE
30. SUDDENLY Susan
31. S.W.A.T.

Word-Find 65

```
N O S D N A D R O F N A S R G
A D L E F N I E S A Q E E V N
W B H C R S S I Z T H M C I I
L E C K Q E S E J S M J O D K
Y U R U R T H K A A S S N L Y
L E A S E A E W H H I X D O K
N R E R P R P E E S U M C G S
E S S C T I G H T S A N I D H
D W R R A D N E T S L S T I I
D A A U E P R C S U I E Y L N
U T T L S K S B I F O L T O D
S G S E A Q U E S T D S V S I
A S A T U R D A Y R Y N A E G
U T E R C E S A V E D B Y R R
P A O S H A N A N A C P Q C A
```

TV GUIDE

TV GUIDE WORD-FINDS

"The Monkees"

1. ANTICS
2. BAND
3. COMEDY
4. DAVY JONES
5. EMMY Award
6. Cult FAVORITE
7. "HERE WE COME…"
8. LOS ANGELES
9. MADCAP adventures
10. MARACAS
11. MICKY DOLENZ
12. MIKE NESMITH
13. MUSIC
14. PETER TORK
15. Fictional POP GROUP
16. QUARTET
17. RERUNS
18. SIXTIES
19. SLAPSTICK
20. Outside SONGWRITERS
21. STRUGGLING band
22. SURREAL
23. SYNDICATION
24. Based on THE BEATLES
25. THEME SONG
26. WOOL HAT

Word-Find 66

```
K P U O R G P O P A C D A M P
W C C S A C A R A M S I B R E
M K I H T T H E B E A T L E S
S R E T I R W G N O S H H R I
H O T M S A U O A Z B E P U X
T T G E M P J G Z N R M L N T
A R I P T Y A F G E A E O S I
H E A M V R R L W L S S S B E
L T T A S S A E S O I O A U S
O E D I W E C U C D P N N R C
O P E F R O N O Q Y D G G E I
W F Z R M O M E X K G A E X T
F G U E R E V A K C R T L P N
A S Y N D I C A T I O N E Q A
C Y E Y Y E B G F M M U S I C
```

TV GUIDE WORD-FINDS

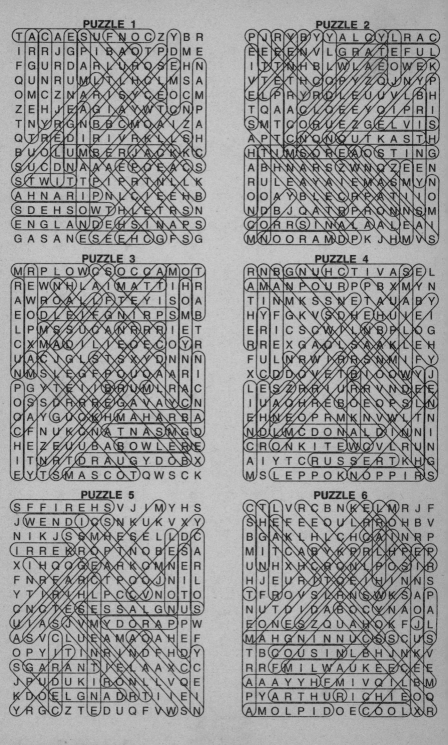

TV GUIDE WORD-FINDS

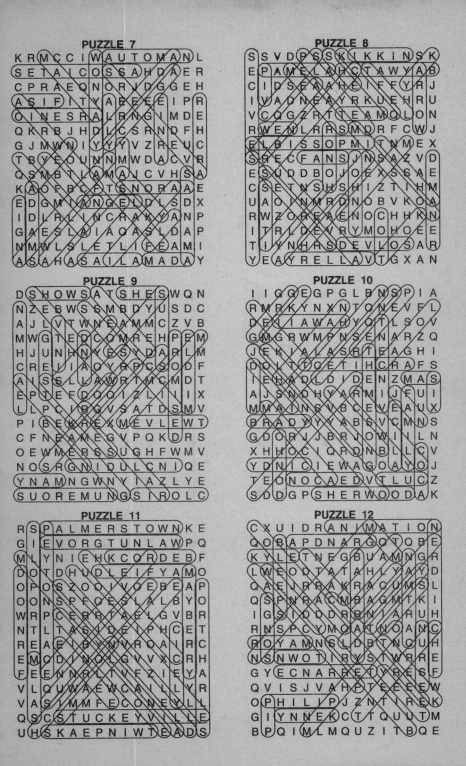

PUZZLE 7

```
K R M C C I W A U T O M A N L
S E T A I C O S S A H D A E R
C P R A E Q N O R I D G G E H
A S I F I T Y A E E E I P R
O I N E S R A L R N G I M D E
Q K R B J H D L C S R N D F H
G J M W N I Y Y V Z R E U C
T B Y E O U N N M W D A C V R
Q S M B T L A M A J C V H S A
K A O F B C F T S N O R A A E
E D G M I A N G E L D L S D X
I D L R L I N C R A K Y A N P
G A E S L A I A O A S L D A P
N M W L S L E T L I F E A M I
A S A H A S A I L A M A D A Y
```

PUZZLE 8

```
S S V D P S S K I K K I N S K
E P A M E L A H C T A W Y A B
C I D S E A A H E I F F Y R J
I V A D N E A Y R K U E H R U
V C Q G Z R T T E A M O L O N
R W E N L R R S M O R F C W J
E L B I S S O P M I T N M E X
S P E C F A N S J N S A Z V D
E S U D D B O J O E X S S A E
C S E T N S H S H I Z T I H M
U A O K N M R D N O B V K O A
R W Z O R E A E N O C H H K N
I T R L D E V R Y M O H O E E
T I Y N H R S D E V L O S A R
Y E A Y R E L L A V T G X A N
```

PUZZLE 9

```
D S H O W S A T S H E S W Q N
N Z E B W S S M B D Y U S D C
A J L V T W N E A M M C Z V B
M W G T E D C O M R E H P E M
H J U N H N Y E S Y D A R L M
C R E L I A O Y R P C S O D F
A N S S L L A W R T M C M D T
E P T E F D O O I Z L I I X
L L P C I R G V S A T D S M V
P I B E R H E X M E V L E W T
C F N E A M E G V P Q K D R S
O E W M E R S S U G H F W M V
N O S R G N I D U L C N I Q E
Y N A M N G W N Y I A Z L Y E
S U O R E M U N G S I R O L C
```

PUZZLE 10

```
I I G G E G P G L B N S P I A
R M R K Y N X N T O N E V F L
D E K I A W A H Y O T L S O V
G M G R W M P N S E N A R Z Q
J E K I A L A S R T E A G H I
D O I T T C E T I I H C R A F S
I E H A D L D I D E N Z M A S
A J S N D H Y A R M I J F U I
M M A I N S V B C E V E A U X
B R A D Y Y Y A B S V C M N S
G D O R J J B R J O W I I L N
X H H O C I Q R D N B L L C V
Y D N I C I E W A G O A O J
T E O N O C A E D V T L U C Z
S D D G P S H E R W O O D A K
```

PUZZLE 11

```
R S P A L M E R S T O W N K E
G I E V O R G T U N L A W P Q
M L Y N I E H K C O R D E B F
D O T D H U D L E I F Y A M O
O P O S Z O O I V O E B E A P
O O N S P F O E S L A L B Y O
W R P C E R R T A E L G V B R
N T L T A S I D E I P H C E T
R E A E I B Y N N V R O A I R C
E M C D I N O L G V V X C R H A
F E E N N R L T V F Z I E Y A
V L Q U W A E W C A I L L Y R
V A S I M M F E C O N E V L L
Q S C S T U C K E Y V I L L E
U H S K A E P N I W T E A D S
```

PUZZLE 12

```
C X U I D R A N I M A T I O N
Q O B A P D N A R G O T Q B E
K Y L E T N E G B U A M N G R
L W E O D T A T A H L Y A Y D
Q A E N P R A K R A C U M S L
Q S P N R A C M B A G M T K I
I G S I D D D R N I A R U H
R N S P C Y M O A T N O A N C
R O Y A M N S L D B T N C U H
N S N W O T I R V S T W R R E
G Y E C N A R R E T Y R E S F
Q V I S J V A H P T E E E E W
O P H I L I P J Z N T I R E K
G I Y N N E K C T T Q U U T M
B P Q I M L M Q U Z I T B Q E
```

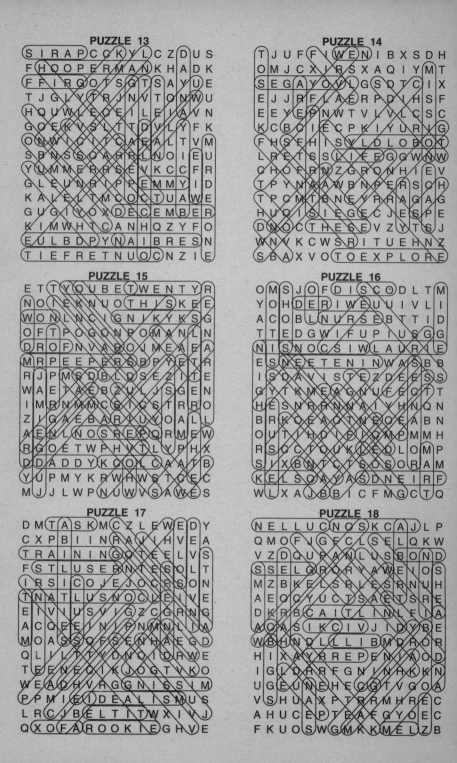

PUZZLE 13

```
S I R A P C O K Y L C Z D U S
F H O O P E R M A N K H A D K
F F I R G O T S G T S A Y U E
T J G L Y T R J N V T O N W U
H Q U W L E O E I L E I A V N
G O E K V S L T T D V L Y F K
O N W I C I T C A E A L T V M
S B N S S O A R R L N O I E U
Y U M M E R H S E V K C C F R
G L E U N R I P P E M M Y I D
K A L E L T M C O C T U A W E
G U G I Y O X D E C E M B E R
K I M W H T C A N H Q Z Y F O
E U L B D P Y N A I B R E S N
T I E F R E T N U O C N Z I E
```

PUZZLE 14

```
T J U F F I W E N I B X S D H
O M J C X I R S X A Q I Y M T
S E G A Y O V L G S D T C I X
E J J R F L A E R P D H S F
E E Y E P N W T V L V L C S C
K C B C I E C P K I Y U R G
F H S F H I S V L D L O B O T
L R E T S S L I F E G G W N W
C H O F R N Z G R O N H I E V
T P Y N A A W B N P E R S C H
T R C M T B N E Y R R A G A G
H U O I S I E G E C J E S P E
D N O C T H E S E V Z Y T S J
W N V K C W S R I T U E H N Z
S B A X V O T O E X P L O R E
```

PUZZLE 15

```
E T T Y O U B E T W E N T Y R
N O I E K N U O T H I S K E E
W O N L N C I G N I K Y K S G
O F T P O G O N R O M A N L N
D R O F N V A R O I M E A E A
M R P E E P E R S B P Y E T R
R J P M S D B L D S E Z I T E
W A E T A E B Z U L J S G E N
I M R N M M C S I O S T R R O
Z I G A E B A R I U Y O A L L
A E N L N O S R E P Q R M E W
R G O E T W P H V T L Y P H X
D D A D D Y K C O L C A A T B
Y U P M Y K R W H W S T C E C
M J J L W P N U W V S A W E S
```

PUZZLE 16

```
O M S J O F D I S C O D L T M
Y O H D E R I W E U U I V L I
A C O B L N U R S E B T T I D
T T E D G W I F U P I U S G G
N I S N O C S I W L A U R X E
E S N E E T E N I N W A S B B
I S D A V I S T E Z D E E S S
G Y T K M E A G N U F E C T
H E S N R A N N A I Y H N Q N
B R K O E A O T N E O E A B N
O U T I H D I E I O M P M M H
R S C C T O U K L E D L O M P
S I X B N T C T S O S O R A M
K E L S O A Y A S D N E I R F
W L X A J B B I C F M G C T Q
```

PUZZLE 17

```
D M T A S K M C Z L E W E D Y
C X P B I I N R A I H V E A
T R A I N I N G O T E E L V S
F S T L U S E R N T E S O L T
I R S I C O J E J O C R S O N
T N A T L U S N O C L E N V E
E I V U S V I G Z C G R N G
A C Q E E I N I P N M N L I A
M O A S S O F S E N H A E G D
Q L I L T T Y D N O I D R W E
T E E N E C I K J O G T V K O
W E A D H V A G G N I S S I M
P P M I E I D E A L I S M U S
L R C J B E L T I T W X I V J
Q X O F A R O O K I E G H V E
```

PUZZLE 18

```
N E L L U C N O S K C A J L P
Q M O F J G E C L S E L Q K W
V Z D Q U R A N L U S B O N D
S S E L G R O R Y A W E N O S
M Z B K E L S R L E S R N U H
A E O C Y U C T S A E T S R E
D K R B C A I T L I N L F I A
A O A S I K C I V J I D Y B E
W B H N D L L L I B M D R O R
H I X A Y R R E P E N I A O D
I G L D A R F G N I N H K K N
U G E U N E H E C G T V G O A
V S H U A X P T R R M H R E C
A H U C E P T E A F G Y O E C
F K U O S W G M K K M E L Z B
```

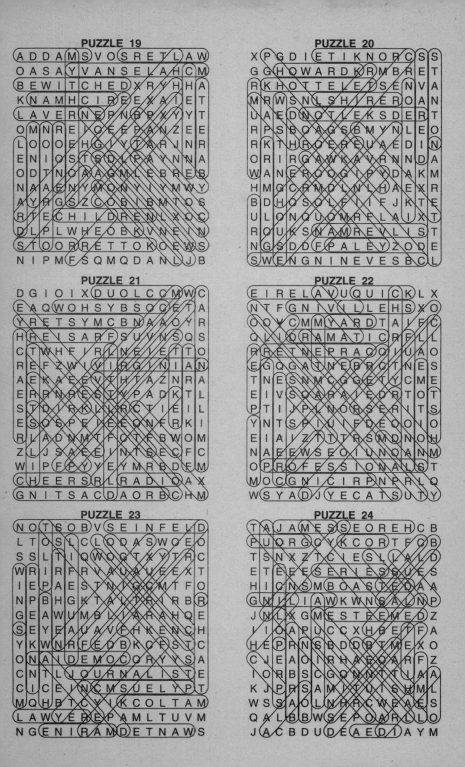

TV GUIDE WORD-FINDS

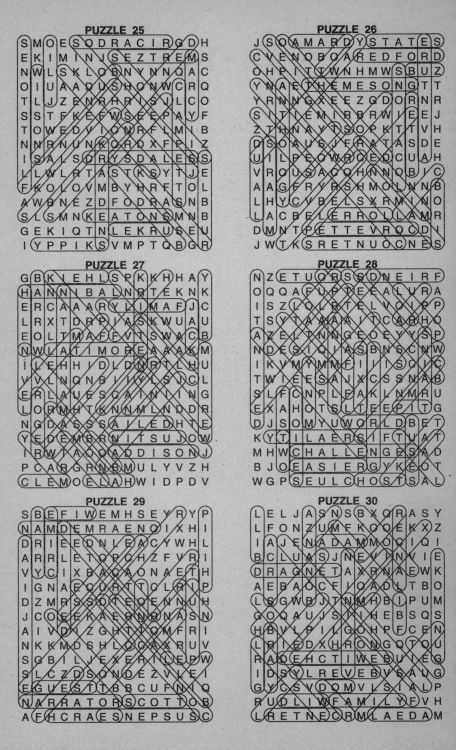

PUZZLE 25

PUZZLE 26

PUZZLE 27

PUZZLE 28

PUZZLE 29

PUZZLE 30

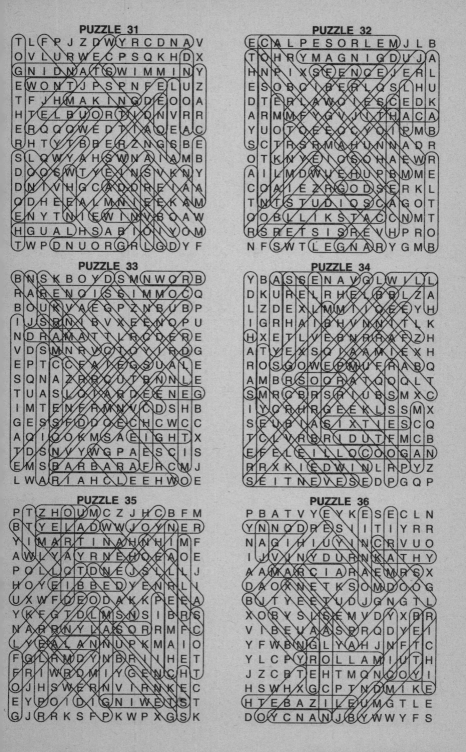

PUZZLE 31

```
T L F P J Z D W Y R C D N A V
O V L U R W E C P S Q K H D X
G N I D N A T S W I M M I N Y
E W O N T J P S P N F E L U Z
T F J H M A K I N G D E O O A
H T E L B U O R T N D N V R R
E R Q Q O W E D T X A Q E A C
R H T Y T B B E R Z N G S B E
S L O W Y A H S W N A I A M B
D O O S W T Y E I N S V K N Y
D N I V H G C A D D R E I A A
O D H E E A L M N F E K A M
E N Y T N I E W I N B O A W
H G U A L H S A B I O N Y O M
T W P D N U O R G R L G D Y F
```

PUZZLE 32

```
E C A L P E S O R L E M J L B
T O H R Y M A G N I G D U J A
H N P I X S F E N C E J E R L
E S O B C I B E R L Q S L H U
D T E R L A W O I E S C E D K
A R M M F Y G V J N T H A C A
Y U O T O E E O C Y O I P M B
S C T R S R M A H U N N A D R
O T K N Y E N O S O H A E W R
A I L M D W U E H U P B M M E
C O A I E Z R G O D S E R K L
T N T S T U D I O S C A G O T
O O B L L I K S T A C C N M T
R S R E T S I S R E V H P R O
N F S W T L E G N A R Y G M B
```

PUZZLE 33

```
B N S K B O Y D S M N W O R B
R A R E N O I S S I M M O C Q
B O U K V A E G P Z N B U B P
I J S R N I B V X F E N O P U
N D R A M A T I L R C D E R E
V D S M N R V C T O Y J R D G
E P T C C F A I E G S U A L E
S Q N A Z R R C U T B N N L E
T U A S L O T A R D E E N E G
I M T E N F R M N V C D S H B
G E S S F D D O E C H C W C C
A Q I O O K M S A E I G H T X
T D S N V Y W G P A E S C I S
E M S B A R B A R A F R C M J
L W A R I A H C L E E H W O E
```

PUZZLE 34

```
Y B A S S E N A V G L W I L L
D K U R E L R H E L B R L Z A
L Z D E X L M M I I Q E E Y H
I G R H A I B H V N N I T L K
H X E T L I V E B N R R A F Z H
A T Y E X S Q L A A M K E X H
R O S G O W E P M U F R A B Q
A M B R S O O R A T Q Q L T
S M R C B R S R I U B S M X C
I Y C R H R G E E K L S S M X
S E U B A S I X T I E S C Q
T C L V R B R N D U T F M C B
E F E L E I L L O C O O G A N
R R X K I E D W I N L R P Y Z
S E I T N E V E S E D P G Q P
```

PUZZLE 35

```
P T Z H O U M C Z J H C B F M
B T Y E L A D W W J O Y N E R
Y I M A R T I N A H N H I M F
A W L Y A Y R N E H O F A O E
P O L L C T D N E J S L L L J
H O Y E I B B E D Y E N R L I
U X W F O E O D A K K P E E A
Y K F G T D L M S N S I B R S
N A P R N Y L A S O R R M F C
L Y E A L A N N U P K M A I O
F G L A M D Y N B R I N H E T
F R I W R D M I Y G E N C H T
O J H S W E R N V I R N K E C
E Y P O I D I G N I W E T S T
G J R R K S F P K W P X G S K
```

PUZZLE 36

```
P B A T V V Y E Y K E S E C L N
Y N N O D R E S I I T I Y R R
N A G I H I U Y I N C R V U O
I J V I N Y D U R N K A T H Y
A A M A R C I A R A E M R S X
D A O X N E T K S O M D C O G
B U T Y E E T U D J G N G T L
X O B Y S L S E M V D Y X B R
V I B E V A A S R Q D Y E I
Y F W B N G L Y A H J N F T C
Y L C P Y R O L L A M I U T H
J Z C B T E H T M Q N C O Y I
H S W H X G C P T N D M I K E
H T E B A Z I L E U M G T L E
D O Y C N A N J B Y W W Y F S
```

TV GUIDE WORD-FINDS

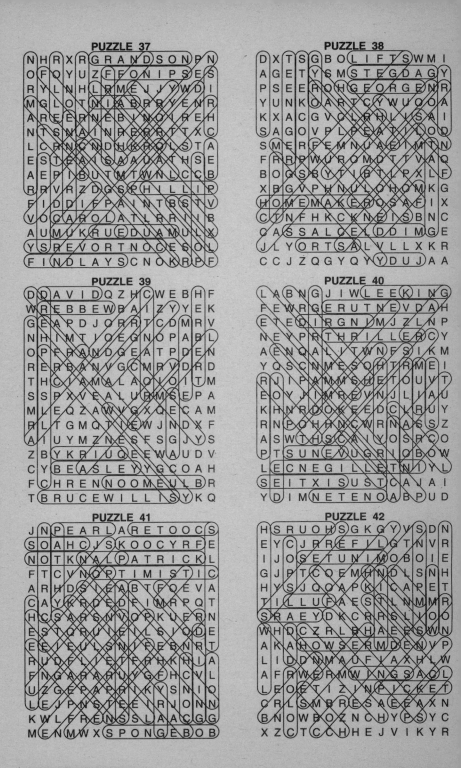

PUZZLE 37

PUZZLE 38

PUZZLE 39

PUZZLE 40

PUZZLE 41

PUZZLE 42

TV GUIDE WORD-FINDS

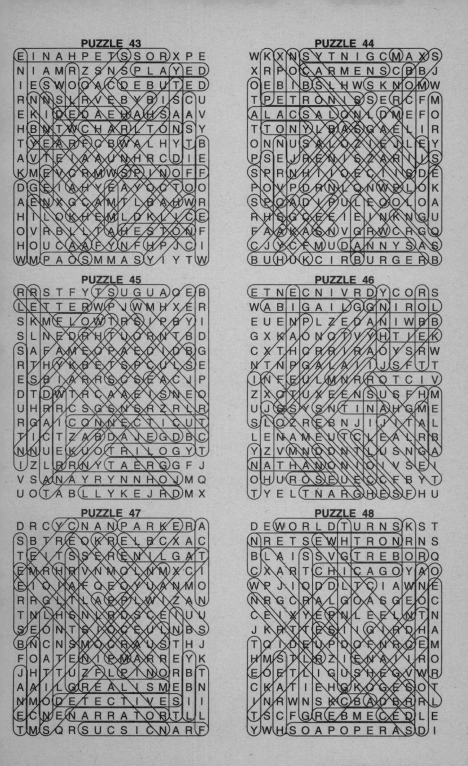

PUZZLE 43

```
E I N A H P E T S S O R X P E
N I A M R Z S N S P L A Y E D
I E S W O O A C D E B U T E D
R N N S L R V E B Y B I S C U
E K I O E D A E H A H S A A V
H B N T W C H A R L T O N S Y
T Y E A R F O B W A L H Y T B
A V T E I A A U N H R C D I E
K M E V C R M W S P I N O F F
D G E I A H Y E A Y O C T O O
A E N X G C A M T L B A H W R
H I L O K H E M L D K L I C E
O V R B L L T A H E S T O N F
H O U C A A F Y N F H P J C I
W M P A O S M M A S Y I Y T W
```

PUZZLE 44

```
W K X N S Y T N I G C M A X S
X R P O C A R M E N S C B B J
O E B I B S L H W S K N O M W
T P E T R O N I S S E R C F M
A L A C S A L O N I D M E F O
T T O N Y L B A S G A E L I R
O N N U S A L O Z I E J L E Y
P S E J R E N I S Z A R I I S
S P R N H I I O E C I I S D E
P O V P D R N L Q N W B L O K
S P O A D I P U L E O O L O A
R H S G O E E I E I N K N G U
F A A K A S N V G R W C R G Q
C J Y C F M U D A N N Y S A S
B U H U K C I R B U R G E R B
```

PUZZLE 45

```
R R S T F Y T S U G U A O E B
L E T T E R W P J W M H X E R
S K M F L O W T R S I P B Y I
S L N E D R H T U O R N T B D
S A F A M E O P A E D I D B G
R T H Y K B E T S P C U L S E
E S B I A R R S O S E A C J P
D T D W T R C A A E I S N E Q
U H R R C S G S N S Z R L R
R G A I C O N N E C T I C U T
T I C T Z A B D A J E G D B C
N N U E K U O T R I L O G Y T
I Z L B R N Y T A E R G G F J
V S A N A Y R Y N N H O J M Q
U O T A B L L Y K E J R D M X
```

PUZZLE 46

```
E T N E C N I V R D Y C O R S
W A B I G A I L G G N I R O L
E U E N P L Z E D A N I W B B
G X K A O N O T V Y H T I E K
C X T H C R R I R A O Y S R W
N T N P G A L A I J S F T T
I N F E U L M N R R O T C I V
Z X O T U X E E N S U S F H M
U J S S Y S N T I N A H G M E
S L O Z R E B N J I J I T A L
L E N A M E U T C L E A L R B
Y Z V M N D D N T L U S N G A
N A T H A N O N I O N V S E I
O H U R O S E U E C C F B Y T
T Y E L T N A R G H E S F H U
```

PUZZLE 47

```
D R C Y C N A N P A R K E R A
S B T R E O K R E L B C X A C
T E T S S E R E N I L G A T
E M R H R V N M O L N M X C I
E I O X A F Q E O Y U A N M O
R R G L T L A P P L W I Z A N
T N L H S N I R O S C E I U U
S E O N T S I O C E U L N B S
B N C N S M O C R A U S T H J
F O A T E N I P M A R R E Y K
J H T T U Z F L P X N O R B T
A A I L G R E A L I S M E B N
N M O D E T E C T I V E S I I
E C N E N A R R A T O R T L L
T M S Q R S U C S I C N A R F
```

PUZZLE 48

```
D E W O R L D T U R N S K S T
N R E T S E W H T R O N R N S
B L A I S S V G T R E B O R Q
C X A R T C H I C A G O Y A O
W P J I Q D D L T C I A W N E
N R G C R A L G O A S G E O C
C E I X Y E P N L E E L N T N
J K A T E S I N G I R D H A
T Q I D E U P D O E N R C E M
H M S T L R Z I E N A I I R O
E O E T L I G U S H E G V W R
C K A T I E H G K O G E S O T
I N R W N S K C B A D B R L
T S C F G R E B M E C E D L E
Y W H S O A P O P E R A S D I
```

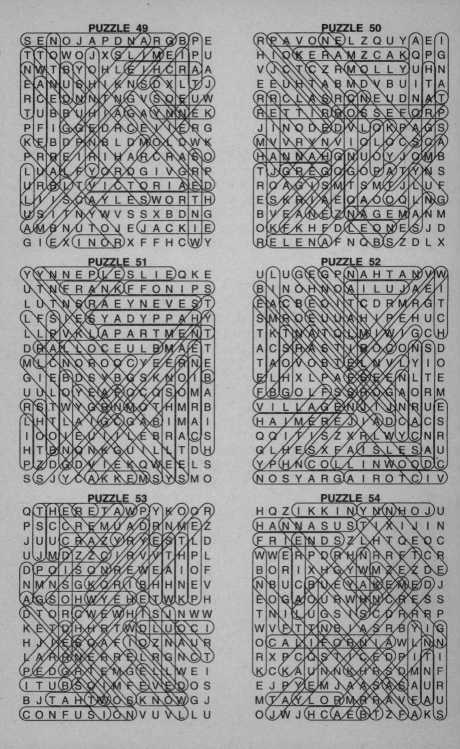

PUZZLE 49

PUZZLE 50

PUZZLE 51

PUZZLE 52

PUZZLE 53

PUZZLE 54

TV GUIDE WORD-FINDS

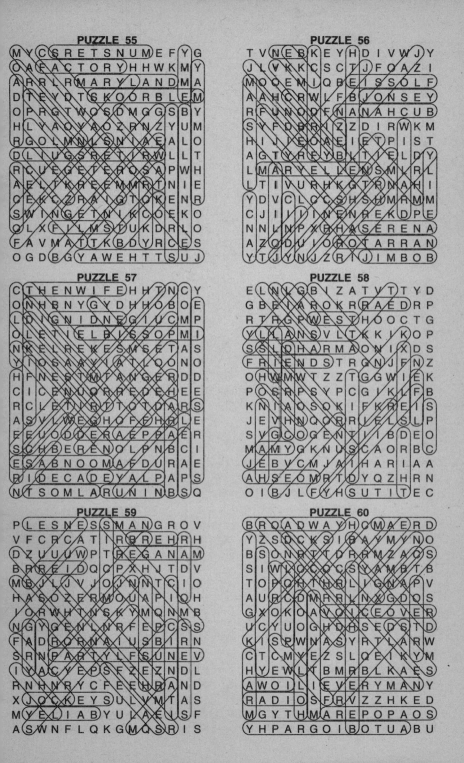

TV GUIDE WORD-FINDS

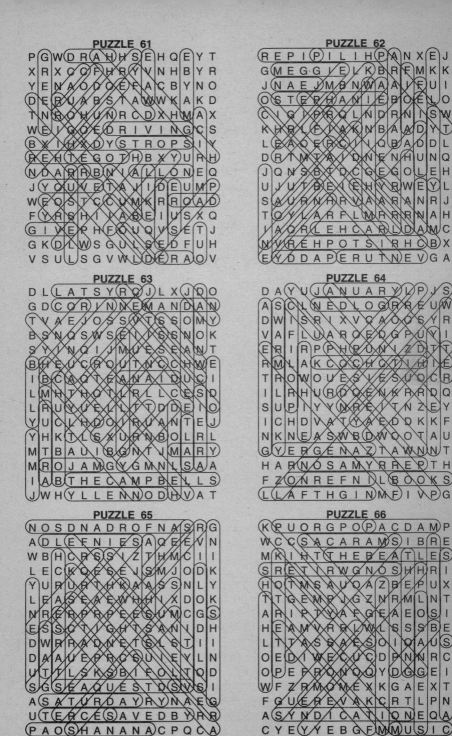

PUZZLE 61

```
P G W D R A H H S E H Q E Y T
X R X C C F H R Y V N H B Y R
Y E N A O D O E F A C B Y N O
D E R U A B S T A W W K A K D
T N R O H U N R C D X H M A X
W E I G O E D R I V I N G C S
B X I H X D Y S T R O P S I Y
R E H T E G O T H B X Y U R H
N D A R R B N A L L O N E Q
J Y O U V E T A I I D E U M P
W E O S T C C U M K R R O A D
F Y R S H I X A B E I U S X Q
G I V E P H F Q U V S E T J
G K D L W S G U L S E D F U H
V S U L S G V W L D E R A O V
```

PUZZLE 62

```
R E P I P I L I H P A N X E J
G M E G G I E L K B R F M K K
J N A E J M B N W A A I F U I
O S T E R H A N I E B O E L O
C I Q I X P R Q L N D R N I S W
K H R L F I A K N B A A D Y T
L E A O E R C I Q B A D D L
D R T M T A I D N E N H U N Q
J Q N S B T D C G E G O L E H
U J U T B E I E H V R W E Y L
S A U R N H R V A A R A N R J
T O Y L A R F L M R R R N A H
I A O R L E H C A R L D A M C
N V R E H P O T S I R H C B X
E Y D D A P E R U T N E V G A
```

PUZZLE 63

```
D L L A T S Y R C J L X J D O
G D C O R I N N E M A N D A N
T V A E J O S S V T S S O M Y
B S N Q S W S E N I S S N O K
S Y I N Q I J M U E S E A N T
B H E U C R O U T N C C H W E
I B C A Q T E A N A I D U C I
L M H T H O T L R L L C E S D
L R U Y U E L L T T D D E I O
Y U C L H D O I R U A N T E J
Y H K T L S X U R N B O L R L
M T B A U I B G N T J M A R Y
M R O J A M G Y G M N L S A A
I A B T H E C A M P B E L L S
J W H Y L L E N N O D H V A T
```

PUZZLE 64

```
D A Y U J A N U A R Y L P J S
A S C L N E D L O G R R E U W
D W I S R I X V C A O O S Y R
V A F L U A R O E D G P U Y I
E R I R P P H R U N I Z D T T
R M L A K C O C H G T N H I E
T R O W O U E S I E S U O C R
I L R H U R D O E N K R R D Q
S U P I Y Y N R E I T N Z E Y
I C H D V A T Y A E D D K K F
N K N E A S W B D W O O T A U
G Y E R G E N A Z T A W N N T
H A R N O S A M Y R R E P T H
F Z O N R E F N I L B O O K S
L L A F T H G I N M F I V P G
```

PUZZLE 65

```
N O S D N A D R O F N A S R G
A D L E F N I E S A Q E E V N
W B H C R S S I Z T H M C I I
L E C K Q E S E J S M J O D K
Y U R U R T H K A A S S N L Y
L E A S E A E W H H I X D O K
N R E R P R P E E S U M C G S
E S S C T I G H T S A N D H
D W R R A D N E T S L S T I I
D A A U E P R C S U I E Y L N
U T T L S K S B I F O L T Q D
S G S E A Q U E S T D S V S I
A S A T U R D A Y R Y N A E G
U T E R C E S A V E D B Y R R
P A O S H A N A N A C P Q C A
```

PUZZLE 66

```
K P U O R G P O P A C D A M P
W C C S A C A R A M S I B R E
M K I H T H E B E A T L E S
S R E T I R W G N O S H H R I
H O T M S A U O A Z B E P U X
T T G E M P J G Z N R M L N T
A R I P T Y A F G E A E O S I
H E A M V R R L W L S S S B E
L T T A S S A E S O I Q A U S
O E D I W E C U C D F N N R C
O P E F R O N Q Q Y D G G E I
W F Z R M O M E X K G A E X T
F G U E R E V A K C R T L P N
A S Y N D I C A T I O N E Q A
C Y E Y Y E B G F M M U S I C
```